Hanging in There

One Man and his Dad take on the Alps in the
World's Toughest Race

Jon R. Chambers

CreateSpace Independent Publishing Platform
ISBN 978-1482354461

To Ali for making it all possible

and

To my Dad for making it all happen

Contents

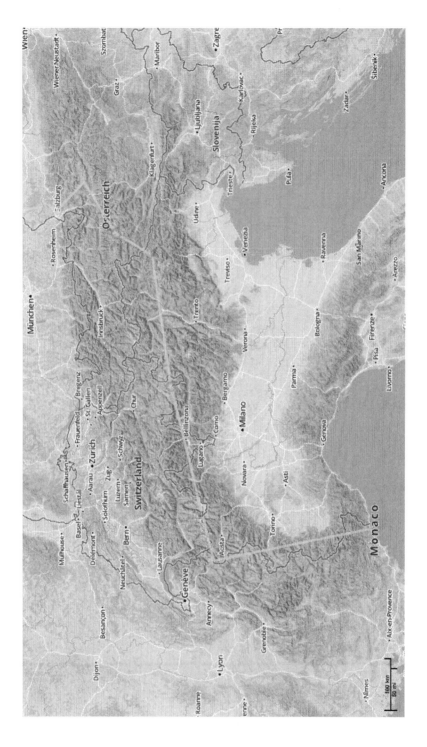

Forward

The Red Bull X-Alps is the world's most extreme race. Just 30 athletes from across the world are selected to take part.

The competitors shoulder their 10kg rucksacks, each one containing a foldable aircraft, in the historic old town of Salzburg in Austria. From here, they run up the nearest mountain to start a two week non-stop adventure that will take them the full length of the European Alps.

Cresting the mountain summit, they will unpack their paragliders and take to the skies, flying as far as they can through sometimes appalling weather conditions. Upon landing, they fold their wings back into their rucksacks and take to the roads and mountain trails, to push on, on foot, non-stop into the night.

The course winds through the highest and most famous mountains in Europe, including the Tre Cime in Italy, the Matterhorn in Switzerland, and of course the mighty Mont Blanc in France to the finish line on the shores of the Mediterranean Sea in the Principality of Monaco.

Over the course of the race, the athletes will cover the distance of twenty marathons on foot and climb the height of Mount Everest four times. They will fly their fragile paragliders to altitudes of over 4000m, through some of the wildest and most remote terrain in Europe. The challenges and dangers are extreme.

Every metre is hard won against the course, the elements, and the increasing mental and physical toll of relentless racing. The pilots are each utterly reliant on their single supporter: a team member solely responsible for keeping the athlete functioning by providing food, overnight shelter and mental support.

From its humble beginnings as a niche paragliding event with just seventeen pilots in 2003, the race has run every other year, growing in both ambition and popularity. Now, over two million extreme sports fans follow the race as it is happens, second by second, on www.redbullxalps.com. The website includes daily high-definition videos, live blogs and interviews with the athletes.

In this book, British athlete Jon Chambers brings you even closer to the action and reveals his personal story of his 2011 race. In doing so he reveals the harsh reality of what it takes to compete in this uniquely demanding challenge: the physical and mental hardship, equipment, extreme conditions, strategic thinking and lucky escapes.

Tom Payne, Geneva, 2012

About this Book

The X-Alps is predominantly a paragliding race so whilst in general I have attempted to avoid using too much paragliding terminology and jargon it has proved impossible to successfully tell this story without using some basic paragliding terms. At the back of the book in Appendix 2 is a section which explains some of the paragliding terms used for non-pilots who are reading this.

Each chapter tells the story of one day in the race and at the start of each chapter is a map detailing the route I took on that day. On each map my starting point is shown with an 'A' and the finishing point for the day is shown with a 'B'. Each day starts with me walking but you can find on the maps symbols indicating the places I launched (a circle with a paraglider) and started flying as well as the places I landed and resumed walking (a circle with a footprint). In some cases, such as where I landed and re-launched in the same place the symbols are superimposed. The line on the maps shows the direct course line between the turn points and the turn point cylinders themselves are also shown. Higher resolution maps are available on my blog (jonrchambers.blogspot.com) if the reader wishes to study the maps in more detail.

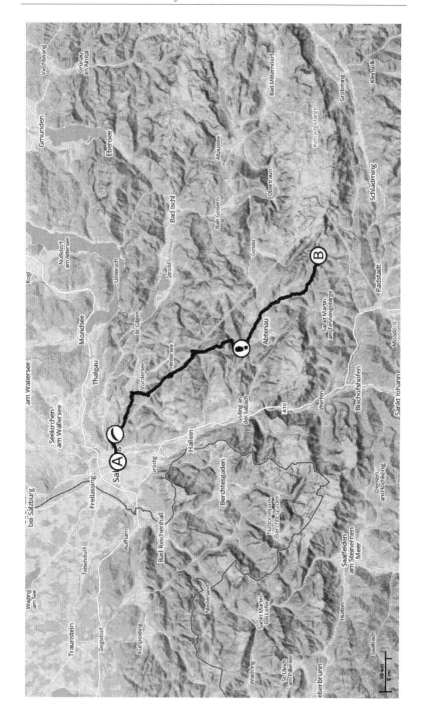

Day 1: Salzburg to the Hofpurglhutte

The idea had been nagging at me for some time. Perhaps years. Thinking back, the first time I really had it in my head that it might be something for me to try was in the summer of 2007. The X-Alps race, which takes place once every two years, took place that year and I toyed with the idea of entering. I wasn't really serious though, at least not then. Scroll forward to 2009 and two friends, Tom and Aidan, competed for Britain. Through them I became a much more avid spectator, glued to the live tracking and even spending time on the phone to Aidan guiding him in Chamonix and, on the final day, trying to find him in the mountains and in the air. So now here I was, standing in the Motzartplatz in Salzburg on July 17th 2011, waiting for the start of the most extreme challenge I'd ever had the audacity (perhaps stupidity) to attempt in my life.

We'd spent the week preceding this moment at the race HQ, going through equipment checks, briefings, press conferences and our own final preparations. We'd had a chance to socialise with the other teams but by the end of the week we just wanted the race to start. The 'we' was my Dad and I, team GBR 2 in the race frequently billed as the World's most extreme. I was the one about to attempt to traverse the entire backbone of the alpine chain by foot and by paraglider. It was, though, my father who had the really tough job. The rules state that each athlete could have one supporter. Dad's job was to do everything necessary to keep me going, including constant food, ensuring I had the right gear with me at all times, planning the route ahead and even keeping me in one piece, physically and mentally. My role may have required more paragliding experience (in my case over 20 years) and being on top physical form (I'd been training for over a year for this) but I was certain that when it came down to the race itself my job was actually simpler. I just had to walk and fly. Dad had to think!

That morning had started early with a final race briefing from Hannes Arch, race mastermind and well known pilot from the famous Red Bull Air Races. In a short speech he talked to us about respect, that he understood what it was like to be a competitor but nevertheless in this race more than any there was a need to respect the race and our own safety. It was appropriate and timely. The road through the centre of Fuschl was practically blocked with team vehicles, crowds of people and the coach (clearly borrowed from the Salzburg ice hockey team the 'Red Bulls') that was to take us to Salzburg. Toma Coconea (ROM), probably the most famous competitor, being one of only 2 people to compete in this race since its inception in 2003, was being cheered and filmed by a throng of avid fans from his home country of Romania. Meanwhile I made my way quietly onto the bus and sat patiently for the day to get going. I was a 'no one' in this race, and to be honest, that's the way I wanted it. My plan was just to quietly get on with it. I'd done my homework. In fact, together with my father we'd spent literally weeks and weeks travelling the route of the race, checking alternatives, calculating height gains and ground distances of alternative paths and buying maps. Lots of maps. The race is 862km from start to finish. At least that is if you follow the straight line between the compulsory 'turn points' spread across Europe's most famous peaks. The reality would of course be different. Not even a paraglider can cross the Alps in a straight line and to complete the race we were more likely to cover double that.

When you've been waiting for something for so long, when it actually comes it almost is a surprise, and so with a few minutes to go we shouldered our packs and wished each other good luck. In this race every competitor has to carry their paraglider, harness, helmet, reserve parachute, emergency flare and instruments with them at all times. For a normal pilot this gear would weigh in around 20kg. We are not normal pilots - our gear is specially made or adapted for this race and most of us are carrying around 10kg. My pack was 9kg. The crowd started counting down along with the announcer and suddenly I realised this was it, we were really going to get started. 5...4...3... as we got closer all I could feel was relief at the waiting finally being over ...2...1... bang! We were off. The run through the streets of Salzburg was manic. Only the first 50m of the route was marked but we were expected to run through the old town in order to satisfy the cameras. Once over the main bridge we were free to choose our own route, and I'd like to say things calmed down a bit. They didn't

Go! The start gun goes off at 11.30am in the Motzartplatz, Salzburg.
Photo: Markus Berger/Red Bull Content Pool

The first leg of the race is from Salzburg up to the summit of the Gaisberg mountain that overlooks the city. This is a famous paragliding site and well known for the Gaisberg race, a classic hill climb for car and motorcycle enthusiasts. It is also the point at which we hoped to get airborne and cover as much of the distance to, and hopefully tag, the next turn point high up on the Dachstein glacier. There are different routes you can take from Salzburg to the top of the Gaisberg, but predominantly we went up the path that leads up the north side. Everyone was running through the city, a side effect of the pent up energy, the crowds, the hype and I'm sure the film crews. In a vain attempt not to overdo that first ascent I'd put my heart rate monitor on. I wouldn't wear it for the rest of the race but I needed it now to ensure I didn't go too fast. It didn't work, as I watched a large part of the field pull away from me I felt compelled to push harder. Film crews and reporters followed us, some on bikes, which did not go down well with law abiding Austrian motorists as we were running for part of it in the opposing direction to the traffic on a one way street.

Out into the suburbs now and things were calming down. Japanese legend and veteran of this race, Ogi, (Kaoru Ogisawa, JPN 1), overtook me on the last stretch of built up road before we left the houses to ascend through the trees. He reached the last junction just ahead of me where a small group of spectators had gathered to cheer their local heroes on (support in Austria was most definitely focussed on the Austrians). The spectators jokingly urged Ogi to take the left fork telling him the leader had gone that way, I knew they were having him on, but the ever trusting Japanese almost switched course before their laughs gave away the joke. Ogi moved out of sight and from that moment on I was on my own ascending the Gaisberg. I really had no idea how many people were in front of me or how many were behind, I just continued up on the paths I'd walked in practise. With a few notable exceptions this was more or less how my race would continue, running my own race, not that I knew it then of course. Interestingly, one of the ironies of the live tracking on the website is that the online spectators frequently knew where I was in the rankings better than I did. I was mostly oblivious to my position relative to the others!

In a further nod to the cameras, the organisers had decided we should all arrive on the summit of the Gaisberg with our national flags draped over our shoulders. In reality I think this was just to make it a little easier for the announcer who was to inform the crowds of who we were. And boy, were there crowds. The take-off area was roped off for us but was surrounded on all but the downhill side with thousands of spectators. I collected my flag at the last junction and traversed across towards the take-off, but before I came out of the trees I passed what looked like it may have once been a fire break, and below me was a group of some of the biggest names in the race, including local legend Helmut Eichholzer (AUT 1), 'Heli' as most people knew him, and Vincent Sprüngli (FRA 1) from France. They'd clearly decided the most efficient route was the direct route despite the undergrowth. Although generally true I decided the going was too tough on this direct line and so had chosen the more traditional zig-zagging path. It seemed my intuition was right as this group had been ahead of me coming out of Salzburg.

It was all irrelevant of course. We'd just spent nearly two hours racing up the Gaisberg and the take-off was more or less still. There was no wind up the slope, no thermal activity, the day was simply too stable. I was early enough to the launch to be able to find a good space and get my wing and harness out and set up. But in hindsight I was anything but relaxed. Every bit of my 20 years of paragliding knowledge told me to be patient and wait, wait for better air, wait for some thermals, but after spending the morning waiting around in the Motzartplatz I was done with waiting. I just wanted to go. I remember seeing Chrigel Maurer (SUI 1), winner from 2009 and clearly the favourite for this race, sitting down eating some pasta provided by his supporter, without even having got his wing out of his bag. I remember thinking even then that the guy had this sorted, totally relaxed and not chomping at the bit like I was. I could have made up many plausible reasons why I should launch, but basically the truth was I just wanted to get away from the crowds. Luckily for me family and friends understood me and the race and were playing a distracting game, my wife called me over to talk to my two daughters and various other excuses were being thought up to try to distract me from preparing to launch. Finally, to a great cheer, Michael Gebert (GER) launched. I have no idea if he was going through the same mental battle as me, but if he was then he caved in, but that may be unfair - he may have just been being brave! Some say that fortune favours the brave, not in this case. We all watched as Michael sank down through the stable air to land at the bottom of the mountain, a disastrous start for such a great competitor. Everyone waited. There was no doubt now that waiting was the right thing to do. Pilots, even the best pilots in the world, will race together in gaggles. Like cyclists we can move faster in groups, in our case due to having more people to find the strongest parts of the climbs in the invisible thermals that are so critical to our progress. Having watched Michael sink out made me realise that in these conditions the only real choice was to fly the first leg with the other competitors. I'd launch with the first group, at the front of it, but with others. This was not a time to take a risk. Ivar Sandsta (NOR), another first timer like myself, was next to crack and took off to an almighty cheer from the expectant crowd. After some painstaking work he finally climbed above the Gaisberg launch. Now, if I was Ivar, I'd have expected to see pilots launching one after the other as soon as I started to climb. We didn't. We just watched him circle slowly, but surely, skywards. Yes it was working but there was no critical gaggle to work together through this first difficult part of the course.

Finally the time had come, pilots were putting on warm weather clothes all over the take-off. Some of the top names were clipping in and ready, and soon we were launching one after the other. I was 3rd or 4th off the mountain in this group, but about half the field launched behind me. I launched easily and soon we were all merrily thermalling away with the TV helicopter flying big circles around us. As always when I compete, the nervousness and the uneasiness I'd been experiencing on the ground flowed out of me and I was now climbing absolutely relaxed, at one with the world and in a gaggle of the world's best pilots. Hang on, more than that, I was near to the top of this gaggle of the world's best pilots. Only Chrigel seemed to be able to stubbornly remain about 20-30m above, somehow untouchable!

Sometimes, flying a paraglider requires patience, with weak climbs and little drift under a blue sky, other flights are more manic, going full speed through strong lift under large and threatening clouds and yet others are plagued by strong headwinds, making everything turbulent and going slow. In this first flight we had all of that in the first 30km! As our gaggle approached the first mountain after the Gaisberg we started to fly around the 'back' of it - to the east side. I have no idea who lead out or why, but despite my instinct saying to go the other way, I stuck religiously with my game plan - fly the gaggle. It worked, although it was touch and go. Finally we were all climbing a couple of kilometres away and level with the north-east end of a ridge. I'm sure we all knew we needed to be on the west face and the clouds told us the going would get better here. I was still near the top but Chrigel was above me. We were circling in more or less nothing, but clearly couldn't glide over the ridge from here. After a while Chrigel left for the mountain on glide and about half the circling column of gliders below me detached and followed him. I waited. It seemed to me that the north face, clearly in shade would not be working and they'd get stuck. Of course, Chrigel, three times Paragliding World Cup champion does not make mistakes, and he flew into lifting air which was just enough to take him effortlessly over the ridge and into a strong climb. Damn and blast! I was now being left behind but it was probably a mistake to push my speed bar to try to catch up as I came into the same north face a 100m or so below the ridge and whilst the lifting air that had taken the breakaway group over was still there, I lost valuable time patiently climbing in this weak lift as I watched pilots climbing away strongly on the other side. Once I was over the ridge I could see that the group above me were now about as high as they could be due to the Salzburg airspace which we were not allowed to enter. Effectively our lead gaggle was now split into two and I was in the second group spiralling skywards in a very powerful climb, completely at odds with the first section of the flight.

As I circled skywards I noticed something my fellow thermallers somehow missed. The lead group, having left at the airspace limit were now all flying with either 'big ears' or in some cases had even stopped to spiral down. It was clear to me that the next kilometre or so of air was all lifting strongly as they were all trying to avoid infringing the airspace. So with 300m still to climb to the airspace ceiling I left to chase the leaders with the speed bar pushed as far as I dared in the rough air. It worked, after a few kilometres of constant lifting air I was less than 100m off of the airspace ceiling and not so far behind this lead group. We were approaching the edge of the airspace where our 'ceiling' stepped up from around 2000m to 3000m. It was at this exact point that the lifting air stopped and the south wind started to blow! Ahead of me a pilot, I think it was Paul Guschlbauer (AUT 4), a very talented test pilot, hit turbulence and his whole wing collapsed as we pushed into the headwind over a ridge. His wing went behind him, coming back in a stall before rotating violently. I've watched many pilots not recover their wing from similar situations and end up throwing their reserve parachute, but it was a testament to his skill that he controlled the wing well and was soon back on course, albeit with significantly less altitude! Nevertheless it was a clear warning and I started flying a bit more carefully. With a strong head wind it is clear that the lift we'd sped through was aided by convergence, what's more the sky above us was full of big clouds spreading out and we knew that a cold front was approaching. This front would bring with it bad weather and so it meant we were in a race against time to cover as much distance as we could before it arrived. Suddenly everyone seemed to scatter and I chose not to take a moderate climb due to the drift being too strong. It turned out to be an error as those that did seemed to fair better pushing south at altitude. I waited patiently but I was more or less on my own now. The Abtenau valley beckoned, and at least I'd be over these ridges onto the south faces with the next glide. Or so I thought. What actually happened was I ended up losing a lot of height pushing into the wind and as I came around a south facing ridge, expecting lift from both the dynamic wind and from thermals I encountered nothing but a windswept hillside. Pushing on I realised I was approaching a tight tree covered valley running north south to my left then turning west in front of me before finally twisting back south to join the main valley system. A wing off to my left was lower than me in the middle of the valley heading south. I was not in a good position but I consoled myself with the fact that he appeared to be in a worse position. How wrong I was. What actually happened was that he continued in a straight line seemingly being lifted effortlessly over the ridge in front, whilst I was pinned on the corner in strong wind and strong sink. I turned and flew down the valley heading west now on the south facing slopes. It seemed logical but it was all wrong, I was sinking like a lead balloon and to make matters worse the valley was unlandable, 'V' shaped and completely lined with trees. I was not going to be able to out glide it either. As I got lower my calm piloting instinct took over. Look for somewhere, anywhere, where I might get the wing down safely. Aha! There it was, a small area of shrubs and small trees on the 45 degree slope near the very bottom of the valley. Now the approach, the wind was all over the place down here, I was well below the tops of the low hill to my south and realised that the wind was mainly blowing down the valley. As I put in a turn to position myself perhaps less than 100m from the bottom of the valley now, I realised there was lifting air on the south side of the valley in the lee of the low hill separating this valley from the main one. Suddenly it all made sense, the strong south wind was rotoring over this hill, and the valley was so narrow that despite it being into wind the slope I'd flown along had strongly sinking air due to the down force of this rotor. Even the apparently lucky fate of my fellow competitor was now obvious, he was low enough to have been carried along the valley in what was basically a back eddy and the final section was lifting due to the updraft from this big rotating mass of air. He'd basically got out of here on the rotor. My situation was much graver though, right down in the bottom of the V-shaped valley it was tough work. Still I now had a way out.

There was no phone signal here, and so my live tracking was no longer sending a signal to the internet site. Little to my knowledge at the time, friends were speeding towards me with tree climbing equipment expecting the worst given my signal showed I had not moved for some time. But I was not out of it yet. Soaring painstakingly up on the rotor I climbed some 300m to get up to near the top of the hill. Nevertheless the final part was too tough, every time I got near enough to try for the ridge the air became very rough and any lifting air was smashed to pieces. I hung on and worked my way along to the west to where the hill dropped away and this side valley joined the main valley. I eased over the shoulder of the hill as though on eggshells but in the end the air was smooth here and I was onto the south face with ease. I had expected to be able to work my way back east along this face to where the ground was higher and a couple of other pilots were climbing out under a worsening sky. I was too low though, and cursed my stupidity for not reading the conditions in that narrow valley better. I landed at the highest point I could before the trees, on the edge of a track that lead back up the mountain, with the intent of walking up and getting back in the air where I felt I should rightfully still have been. After a short phone chat with Tom

Payne, veteran of the 2009 race and our team's weather man and strategic advisor, it was very clear I was not thinking straight. The bad weather would beat me to the top and my walk up would be wasted. I was learning about X-Alps tactics. It was a steep learning curve. Now I had to walk down into the valley that moments ago I could have simply glided down into.

It was here that my race preparation kicked in. I knew the most efficient walking route from here to the slopes of the Dachstein. After a quick short cut down to the valley floor (first rule of walking in the X-Alps - never walk round a field if cutting across it is quicker!) I joined the route I knew and set off striding along the valley floor. After a while I saw a car parked up ahead and some 30m off the road to my right, in the middle of a field, were an elderly couple sitting on camping chairs staring at the sky. He shouted to me something in German, which I could not understand. I shouted back to them that I was English. He clearly didn't speak much English but that was not going to dampen his excitement in sharing his news with me which he did in a sort of mixed up Anglo-German tongue of his own devising. Despite the incomprehensible language we seemed to have just created I understood him perfectly. He was excitedly waving at a couple of gliders still in the air over the hills to the north of us and relaying to me that some pilots were trying to fly from Salzburg to Monaco. "I know" I replied, "I'm one of them" to which they started cheering and clapping me. What a remarkable following this race has!

By late afternoon the front hit, along with strong winds and rain. I stopped briefly for food which my Dad had prepared and assessed the situation. The roads loop away to the south west here but I needed to head south east into the Dachstein Mountains for the second turn point. The first challenge was that heading in this direction meant leaving the road network, and therefore access to my supporter and it would not be possible to reconnect before the compulsory rest period (11pm to 4am) took effect. We hatched a plan, which involved walking to the Hofpurglhutte, a mountain hut at over 1700m. From there I still had two further choices to make the Dachstein turn point the next morning, heading still higher to the Ademek hut before crossing the glaciers to the north of the official turn point, or continuing to traverse along the south west faces before heading up the path under the Dachstein cable car. We needed to choose as the first option would require either a mountain guide or a fiendishly difficult *via ferrata* in order to avoid crossing a section of glacier full of crevasses. Time was ticking and I did not have time to stop and discuss these options with my father so I set off towards the hut pushing hard in order to ensure I made it before 11pm, but at the same time talking on my phone to my Dad to fix the plan for the next section. Although the high route across the glaciers was more direct, I had not lined up a mountain guide and we soon realised that mobilising a guide for a 6am start the next day from the Ademek hut would be a challenge given it was already 9pm. Furthermore with the front passing through there would most likely be fresh snow on the glacier making the going slow. The route round to the south side was by contrast longer, but rather more certain, and mostly at a lower altitude. Finally we elected to take the latter option to avoid the glacier crossing.

As darkness came the wind was howling, strengthened by the front and the fact I was now much higher and very exposed on a mountain spur. Earlier, as I'd set off on the walk up, the signs told me it would take about 4hrs, but I only had 3 to walk it in, so I dared not slow down. The rain came and went and so I was walking most of the time with a poncho covering me and my pack but from time to time the wind would get underneath it and try to blow it off over my head. It was incredibly annoying but I had no alternative. My path up joined a footpath that traversed across to the hut, by now the signposts were telling me it was about an hour to the hut, and it was not even 10pm, so I knew I could make it easily and started to relax. It was now extremely dark and as I came round some small bushes some shapes started lumbering towards my head torch. More shapes appeared and the lumbering turned into running, soon I was more or less surrounded by a herd of cows, attracted by my head torch. It may sound silly but the situation spooked me – these huge animals were pushing and jostling and as I tried to get away from them they just started to follow me, if I sped up they'd break into a trot and then a run. I realise cows are not aggressive, but in the dark on the mountain side I was seriously concerned about being accidentally trampled by these beasts. I turned off my head torch and started to move as quickly as I could. It was pitch black and I lost the path doing this but it seemed to work, sort of, as without the light the cows slowed down, although still following hesitantly. As I traversed around the hillside I knew the path was below me so I picked my way down and re-found it. At the same point I saw more huge shapes blocking the path in front of me. Oh great, I thought, but somehow these shapes seemed different, and drawing closer to them I realised the cows had stopped some way behind – these new shapes turned out to be horses and they did not seem in the least bit interested in me. Furthermore the cows seemed wary of them and so once again I found myself walking across the high mountains in the dark on my own.

Arriving at the hut was a relief. I had a vision of warm food and drink and a bunk for the few hours of sleep I'd grab. Walking in, I arrived at a sort of reception. The Austrian man who greeted me looked like he'd just audition for Gollum in the Lord of the Rings. Balding but at the same time with long lanky hair he looked like he'd been separated from society for too long, living up here in the mountains. He didn't speak much English so we communicated by words rather than full sentences. I mentioned the race hoping it would aid the process, but he'd never heard of it so that didn't help my cause. I was exhausted and I couldn't cope with trying to sort this out, as simple as getting a bunk for the night in a mountain hut is,

I'd somehow forgotten about it on the way up and just
expected to eat and then drop into a bunk and sleep. The first
problem we quickly established was that the kitchen was closed
– there was no food available. Secondly it was late and being
the height of summer the hut was pretty full and most of the
people were already snuggly wrapped up in their bunks fast
asleep. I must of looked a fairly sorry sight too – damp,
bedraggled and carrying ridiculous equipment (who carries a
paraglider into a mountain hut in the middle of the night in
dreadful weather?). After some discussion with a lady who I
assumed was his wife they established there was a free bunk in
room 15. I mentioned that I'd be leaving at 4.30am to check
that the hut wasn't closed up completely at night or anything
but that only resulted in a whole new round of discussion
between him and his wife. Apparently this room had small
children in and they didn't want me to wake them up now and
then again at 4.30. The decided I could sleep out in the 'winter
hut', a separate building where he told me there was plenty of
space. By now I think the realisation of what I was attempting
had, for a small part at least, sunk in and he refused to take
payment for the stay and gave me a bottle of water and big bar
of chocolate, which I very gratefully took from him.

I made my way across to the other building and realised
that the wind had picked up further – it was really quite grim
out now. As I came into the hut there was a small entrance area
with two doors leading off, I assumed one would go downstairs
as the hut was on a slope but it seemed to only be a
rudimentary toilet. I opened the other door into the bunk room
and people groaned and rolled around in their beds, as people
are inclined to do when someone shines a bright head torch
into what had previously been a peaceful and pitch black room.
The bunks all seemed to be full, and I quickly realised I had no
sleeping bag in any case, except for my glider and I didn't fancy
trying to sort this out in a room full of half-asleep grumpy
people. I'd run out of energy – I looked around for another
solution to see a metal ladder leading up the wall to a big loft

area — aha — there must be more bunks up there and I was hoping they would be empty. I hauled myself up through the hole and found myself in a loft area that was not insulated, with the wind blowing through the rafters and no bunks. There was only a big pile of blankets.

I no longer had the will to try to find a better option, so I just laid about 5 blankets down to make a rudimentary mattress. I then changed out of my damp T-shirt and pulled the one dry item of clothing I still possessed out of my pack – a Red Bull X-Alps hooded fleece and put this on. I realised I was very cold from just this short time faffing around in the hut, so I quickly took off my shoes, pulled about half a dozen blankets on top of me, ate half the chocolate, set my alarm for 4.30am and lay down to sleep. As the wind whistled through the eaves of the building I pulled the hood tighter round my head to try to stay out of the icy draft. It only partially worked as I slept fitfully.

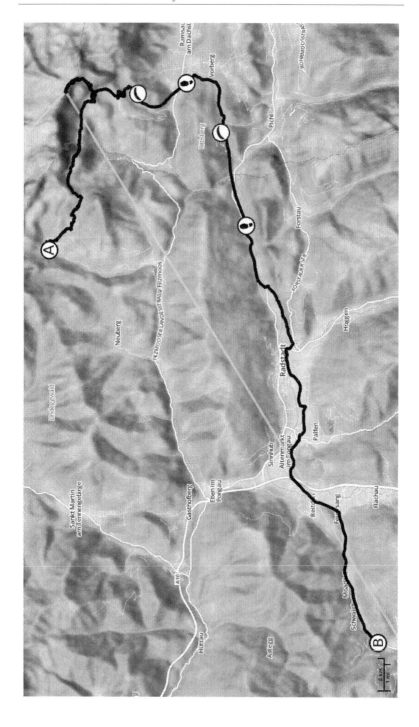

Day 2: Hofpurglhutte to Moos

Often when people have a difficult problem to solve the say, 'let me sleep on it'. I've never understood that expression until this day. Somewhere between being chased by cows and sorting out my lodging the night before I'd made a plan with my Dad – he'd park up in the parking at the road head down below in the valley to the south of the hut. I'd planned to set off from the hut nice and early and continue on the path that traversed around the mountain side towards the 'Sudwandhutte', meanwhile he'd head up a path that bisected this one and we agreed a rendezvous at 5.30am. He was to bring a flask of hot coffee, loads of food and dry, warm clothes. Somehow this plan had not felt right, but, in my state the night before I could not put my finger on what it was.

At 4am I was awake, it had not been the plan but my uncomfortable bed was not conducive to trying to get another thirty minutes sleep so I decided to get on my way. In a sudden moment of clarity I realised the quickest route was not the one we'd planned the night before but the path that led straight down the mountain to exactly where my father was and back up the other side. I didn't even need to get the map out to verify it, I just knew it. We'd spent so long trying to work out the quickest route through these mountains in training that the map was more or less etched on my brain. The reality was that even though staying high and contouring round seemed like the obvious route, it was in fact a lot longer and I knew from having walked it in training that it was a surprisingly slow path

– whilst it looked like it contoured round on the map in reality it was very slow going – picking across scree slopes and boulder fields and scrambling up and down streams that crossed the path. By going down and up I'd save a lot of distance and probably wouldn't lose out too much on additional height gain.

I pulled on my damp and cold clothes, ate more of the chocolate and set off down the mountain with renewed vigour. I had a new plan and it was the right one. I'd sent my Dad a text before leaving to tell him he didn't have to ascend 800m up the mountain to meet me. As first light came to the mountains I could see our team van below me. Soon I was gobbling my breakfast dressed in dry clothes and gulping down hot coffee. I felt refreshed, ready to take on the mountains once again. I was on my way to the Dachstein.

The walk was tough and we'd agreed a new meeting place at the Sudwandhutte, about three hours on. From there it was about two hours to the glacier and the turn point, however my Dad was concerned he'd slow me down heading up to the Dachstein so instead pushed on ahead to meet me at the bottom of the *via ferrata* – the metal safety line and ladder that lead directly up the last part of cliff to the cable car station at 2700m. He was carrying with him the harnesses and climbing equipment we needed to ascend this section, as well as the obligatory dry clothes, given the continuing rain. It seemed my poncho was not really doing the job! Damp rain clouds rolled in and out so that visibility would often drop to near zero. My morale was low as I pushed up the mountain from the Sudwandhutte, I'd fixed my mind on meeting my Dad at the hut but now he'd continued up and I had to do this section on my own I was feeling alone. I passed two other athletes trudging down in the rain, the joy of seeing a familiar face was momentary, as it seems we had no energy for words beyond the most basic of nods and grunts of recognition. Everyone was suffering. My phone rang, and answering through my Bluetooth earpiece (what a brilliant idea this was – allowing me to talk and continue walking with my sticks) I spoke with my Dad. He did not bring good news... he was calling to tell me he'd lost the path somewhere high on the mountain. His purpose was of course well intended – to let me know I needed to pay attention and keep on the path as the visibility became very poor. He reassured me he'd work his way across to the base of the cliff until he regained the path. Nevertheless the effect on me was devastating – a wave of despair washed over me. Whilst there was no tangible reason for this, mentally he was my life line, the rock I was depending on, and somehow now he was lost in the cloud on a dangerous part of the mountain and without him I wouldn't be able to ascend the *via ferrata*.

Whether rationality returned, or whether I just continued trudging on up the mountain simply because there was nothing else to do, I don't know. He did find the path again, of course, and was waiting at the foot of the *via ferrata* as I arrived. It was now excruciatingly cold and I pulled off my wet clothes and redressed in dry clothes, and this time in to a waterproof instead of the poncho. The rain was falling as sleet as I pulled on my climbing harness and shouldered my backpack for the last push up the cliff. As I began to work my way along the metal cable I became aware that my bare hands were completely exposed. The sleet had now turned to proper snow and I stopped once more to pull out my flying gloves from my pack. I realised my Dad had no gloves, and I almost felt guilty continuing up whilst he followed me with what must have been freezing cold hands. Far from holding me back, he had to give me constant encouragement from behind me, mentally pushing me up the mountain. Finally we came out onto the glacier and walked the short distance to the official 'turn point' two flags set in the snow, lost in the cloud. Remarkably it wasn't too windy here, if it wasn't for the cloud we could have launched. But what wind there was was cutting through me like a knife and I was shaking with cold. My Dad tried to shelter me from the worst of the wind whilst I decided what to do next. A quick call to Tom and I decided to wait for a flyable window. Two other pilots, Honza Rejmanek (USA) and Heli were there too, Honza was already in his harness ready to lay out his wing if needed. Independently but simultaneously we all decided to walk the short distance to the restaurant at the cable car station to warm up.

Grim conditions on top of the Dachstein Glacier.
Photo: Chris Hoerner/Red Bull Content Pool

For me this was essential. Still, it felt somehow surreal stepping into a normal room, it was warm and comfortable as I sat down and a great bowl full of warm thick red soup was put in front of me. It was slightly spicy and had a few bits of gristle in it but apart from that I had no clue as to what flavour it was supposed to be, but it didn't matter, it was perfect, exactly what I needed. There was a surprising amount going on in the restaurant on this bleak day, but I soon realised most of it was linked to the race. In the corner sat Jurgen, the race safety director, following the live tracking on the computer in order to check each teams approach and ensure their safety. A number of other locals employed as marshals came in and out and there were multiple film crews and photographers. Other than that there were a few supporters waiting for their athletes to arrive from which ever route they'd chosen . Honza looked somewhat out of place still in his flying harness.

The cloud was coming in and out, but I wasn't too worried about being here in the restaurant as there was still a complete covering of cloud in the valley below. Nevertheless the weather cleared out here on top of the glacier and we had a view across to the launch. Just as I was in the middle of talking by phone to Hugh Miller, the race reporter, I saw Mike Kung (AUT 3) launch. As he wasn't there when I'd been at the launch only a few minutes earlier he must have just arrived, seen the light winds and the take-off clear, thrown out his wing and launched. I was pretty shocked as I knew there was still complete cloud cover below us and running to the window of the cable car station (as did everyone else) this was confirmed.

I polished off the soup in double quick time and rushed back to the take-off behind Honza and Heli and got my glider ready to launch. There were marshals on the take-off obviously in contact with Jurgen in the restaurant as they informed us that if we launched with a complete layer of cloud below us it would be considered cloud flying and we'd be penalised as such. To me this was the right call (I had no intention of flying down through a thick layer of cloud) but staggeringly inconsistent as we'd all just seen Mike take off in exactly this situation. When I queried this sometime later in the race I was told there was no clear evidence that this was the case. This was true if you don't count half a dozen eye witnesses, including the race safety director or the film footage recorded of his launch!

Nevertheless we were on the take-off and miraculously a gap did open in the cloud below us. It wasn't big, but it was big enough, the valley was clearly visible. Honza checked with the marshals that they would not penalise him for launching now, which they couldn't answer, so he launched anyway. He flew out in light winds. I dithered momentarily as I made my final preparations, then pulled up my wing perhaps a minute after Honza. Whether it was tiredness, nervousness or if the wind did really pick up at that exact point I don't know. I do know I was heavy handed with the wing and pulled up too hard, it lifted me off the ice as it over flew me and dumped me back down again. Drat. Heli was now throwing his glider out next to me in an obviously strengthening wind. What followed was frustrating and scary. Heli picked up his wing which came up sideways in the now strong turbulent wind on the cliff edge – he was dragged basically over me – I hit the deck and he jumped me as he flew sideways across the ice. I then tried but couldn't do much better. The conditions were horrid and we were on ice. We were simply skating around, in a wind that was clearly too strong. It then howled. From perhaps 20-30 km/h when Honza had launched we now had over 60 km/h. Both Heli and I were in difficult situations, clipped in to 20 square meters of fabric in a howling gale. Luckily for us there were the marshals there that the race organisation had provided. Unluckily for me they were all local Austrians who had only one interest – see that their local hero was looked after. To that end the three marshals where helping Heli get his wing under control, and then holding it for him – one in the centre and one on each wing tip. Only a lone camera man took pity on me as he saw me getting dangerously dragged across the ice near the cliff edge, however, he was also holding a large and obviously expensive TV camera which was, understandably, his first priority to protect, so his ability to help was somewhat limited. Wings back under control we now stood side by side on the launch with the wind howling, brakes held behind our backs. Heli still had his three assistants whilst I was again on my own now. I commented to Heli that it helped to be Austrian. Heli is a great guy and a genuinely nice person. Clearly in the heat of everything happening he had not been aware of the bias towards him, but now that we were standing there side by side and I made the remark he realised and pointedly told the marshals that they had to help me too. It was a genuinely kind intervention that made absolutely no difference at all.

As we stood there in the strong winds Heli gave it another go, pulling his wing above his head it hauled him off his feet. The glider crabbed to the right now some 20m off the ground but he was going backwards now. He was into his harness being thrown around like a ragdoll, and I wondered if he was going to push the speed bar. I was filled with dread as I watched him on his high performance wing (he was flying the highest performance production wing in the world), stuck in the compression going backwards. Thankfully the wing did not collapse and as he went back out of the lift zone he landed back on the glacier at almost exactly the same time as couple of pilots arrived from the north route. I think it was Vincent Sprüngli who was there to grab his rear lines and dump the wing for him safely as he came down. Although I hardly needed confirmation that I needed to wait for the wind to calm down again this was certainly a stark reminder. My wing was slower than his!

So still on launch and still waiting. Finally the wind calmed down but the gap in the cloud was gone, it was clagged in below us thicker than ever. I'd arrived at the turn point on the glacier somewhere in or near the top ten, but I'd wasted nearly three hours up there waiting for the weather. In that time half the field had come and gone, continuing down the mountain ahead of me. Finally I decided to head back down on the *via ferrata*. I had nothing to show for my time other than a damp and dirty glider from all those drags across the ice.

Although we'd thought through most of the scenarios on the Dachstein, this wasn't our finest hour as far as team logistics went. And it was mostly my fault. The meeting with Dad at the bottom of the *via ferrata* with the harness and climbing gear was perfect as was his accompanying me to the top, however, in my cold and numb state when I changed my clothes at the start of the *via ferrata* I'd forgotten that I had my Bluetooth earpiece in my ear. Pulling off damp clothes had obviously changed that despite my obliviousness to it at the time. So realising that a rather expensive (and also rather small) earpiece was at the bottom of the *via ferrata* narrowed our options. Ideally Dad would have stayed with me whilst I'd tried to launch (it sure would have helped) and then taken the cable car back down. This wasn't possible because he needed to head down the path to try to find the proverbial needle in a haystack, or in this case an earpiece in a boulder field. This also meant he couldn't risk waiting for me, as if I did fly he'd be stuck halfway up a mountain whilst I was miles away, it would be many hours before we'd be able to meet up again. This also complicated matters somewhat because he also had to decide what to do with my *via ferrata* gear. If I'd been successful launching then I wouldn't have needed it, furthermore I probably couldn't fit it in the harness in any case. We finally hit on the smart idea of leaving the gear in the restaurant with the marshals. So as I set off back down the mountain I had to swing by the restaurant once again in order to pick up the harness.

A call to my Dad fixed the plan and remarkably he informed me that he'd found the earpiece. We'd meet again at the Sudwandhutte at the bottom of the path. Once I was disconnected from the cable at the base of the cliff I set off down the path that zigzagged across the scree slopes. Above me Heli was following and he'd obviously decided that scree sliding the direct line would save time. He at least had the good sense to shout '*Achtung!*' as a rock the size of car wheel went careering past me bouncing and crashing its way down the mountain!

Finally, arriving at the hut I found my father having a cup of tea. Well less a cup, more like a bucket – he had asked for a large one and it certainly lived up to the description! I gratefully helped by consuming some of the hot liquid, but even between us we couldn't finish it. I was desperate to keep moving given I'd wasted too much time already. The lower level of cloud engulfed the hut, but I learnt there were three pilots a little below on a spur waiting to launch. I was not convinced that it would be possible to launch here given the cloud, so I continued further down on foot. Several hundred

meters below the hut I came out of the cloud and looking
across in the direction these other pilots were apparently
waiting all I could see was cloud. Finally, I thought, I'd made
the right choice, but then to my shock the cloud seemed to part
before my eyes and out of the thin wispy cloud sailed a glider
heading out into the valley. I couldn't believe it; they'd been in
the right place at the right time and found a gap. I was too low
now and it did not make sense to try to get back up and round
to where they had launched from so I continued down. Above
the bottom car park for the cable car there was a clearing and I
walked up onto this slope to take off and fly out from here.
Heli was laid out a hundred or so meters away to my right as I
looked down the mountain. When I arrived the area was mostly
clear and there was a little cloud blocking the valley in front,
but not much. I laid out in almost nil wind. As I looked down I
realised I could no longer see the valley – it had clouded in. No
matter, I thought, a short wait and I'm sure it'll be fine again.
Instead it started to rain.

This was getting silly. With cloud in front obscuring the
valley I wasn't prepared to launch. I couldn't tell how thick it
was and I didn't know the lie of the land. Heli did launch and
flew out through the cloud. Grumpily I packed up and walked
further down the mountain. On the map I could see another
mountain hut that was on a spur, lower down and less likely to
be affected by this low cloud that was accumulating at the
valley heads. On the map there appeared to be a small clearing
below the hut and I figured it was only about 20mins walk away
and therefore a better bet than staying here. As I set off down I
found that indeed the cloud was very thin and I was soon out
of it. Frustrated that for potentially the third time today I'd
missed an opportunity to fly, I quickened my pace. I arrived at
the hut and walked round onto the spur. All manner of
expletives exploded in my head. There was nowhere to launch.
No matter how much I willed the trees to not be in the way
they were stubbornly positioned so as to render a take-off
under paraglider impossible. I was desperate, but I had to find

something.

Contouring on a little further I suddenly realised I could see the valley below me to my right. With my heart pounding I realised this gap in the trees was probably wide enough to get off the ground. It was quite steep which would help given there was no wind. Dropping my sack I realised there were two issues. Firstly there was actually some wind. It was very light, but what there was was blowing down the slope. Secondly there was one tree at the top where ideally I needed to start from. If I started lower the gap became too narrow. The only choice I had was to go above it and to the side which meant literally laying out underneath another tree, offset versus the gap below. I'd count on the fact as I ran forwards and the wing came up I'd move out from under the tree at the same time, but I'd then also need to correct to the right to line up with the main gap. It was going to be tight, that was for sure. At least there was no cloud to be concerned with.

Clipped in, I set off with a committed run; the wing felt like it snagged on a root momentarily but then it was free and above me. I was running hard with trees flying past but, thankfully, exactly on the right trajectory, and then, finally, I was airborne. It was only a top to bottom flight but it had been hard-earned. I felt relief and exhilaration as I skimmed along the tree covered slopes and round a few wisps of clouds. As I came out into the main valley I headed towards Ramsau, squeezing out the glide as far as I could. As I cleared the last line of trees I realised that the field my glide angle had brought me to was in fact the official landing field. It was complete with windsock telling the direction of the light wind. An auspicious sign – perhaps my luck was turning!

I'd flown more or less due south, which was not exactly on the direct line, but I had a trick up my sleeve. By passing this way into the valley to the south of me I could take advantage of the main valley being some 500m lower than this one with a simple glide down. After a relatively short walk I was coming through a low col on a forestry track with the valley spread out below me. The only challenge now was to find a take-off. The track forked and I started ascending, to my left were open fields, but the slope was very shallow. There was no wind here and I decided that this was the right point to launch. I couldn't really see what was below but I knew the ground dropped away after the field.

I started paragliding 20 years earlier. In those days the performance of the wings was such that you needed a strong wind to stay airborne on an into wind slope. The glide angle of those early gliders was only about half the glide angle of our high performance machines of today. As I prepared my gear to launch I reflected on the fact that this wouldn't even have been a viable launch option in those early days, the field simply wasn't steep enough to ensure that I'd have been able to get airborne!

Another concerted run and I was off the ground, skimming along only a meter or so above the green grassy field, past the trees on my right and then out into the valley. With a proper view of the valley below me I could see now that there was a section that was forested, and I was not sure I'd be able to out-glide it. Every kilometre counted in this race so with my hands tucked behind my risers to reduce drag, I tried to maximise my glide. My luck had finally changed as I dropped lower into the valley a tailwind became apparent, which carried me easily over the forest and a few fields further. As I packed up next to a railway line a man appeared on a mountain bike. Having seen me land on the live tracking he'd come out to say hello. He went on to tell me about the other X-Alps pilots who had landed in almost exactly the same place earlier in the day. Just what I needed – someone reminding me how many places I'd slipped down the rankings due to my dithering on the Dachstein!

For the rest of the late afternoon and evening there was nothing much to do except walk along the road in the direction of St Johan im Pongau and although I never stopped to look at the live tracking, I had a vision of all the athletes strung out along this valley. It had been damp and grey the whole day and as I passed by Ranstad a heavy shower soaked me one more time, as though the weather was just having one last bit of fun for the day. It didn't dampen my spirits though, somehow with the Dachstein turn point now firmly behind me I was full of confidence, I was on the move again and it felt good. As the shower cleared out the setting sun appeared for the first time that day and I recorded my video diary with a brilliant rainbow lighting up the sky behind me.

As the light began to drain from the sky I approached a speed radar on a quiet stretch of road, it was particularly sensitive as the screen announced I was doing a steady 6 km/h as I approached it. A small thing, but it made me smile. I walked on into the night trying to make up for the lost time earlier in the day. Finally we stopped for the night at a small junction opposite a youth hostel.

More by luck than judgement we'd stopped at the highest point on this road – from here the road dropped down to St Johan still about 10km further on. There was a height difference of about 300m between us and the main valley. 300m is equal to 3km when gliding on a paraglider. 3km is 30mins walking, perhaps more if you take the winding road into account. Seeing this I immediately realised I needed to fly this valley. And so a plan was born. The next morning I'd walk up the hill above me (only about 500m ascent) and then launch and glide through this valley at first light. Despite being in a lowly position I climbed into my bunk with the confidence of a man with a plan.

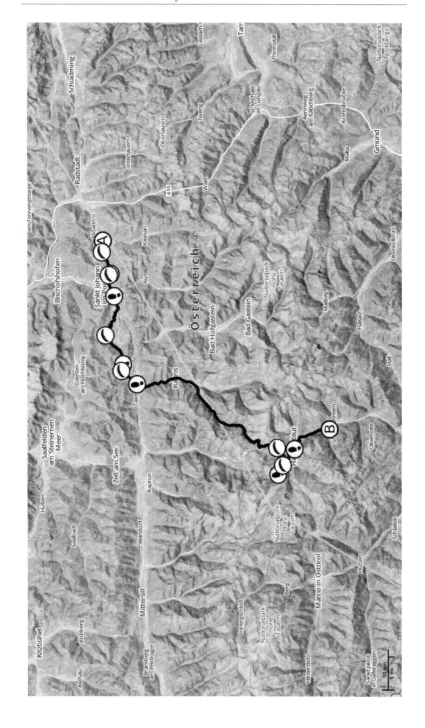

Day 3: Moos to Grosskirchheim

The alarm woke me from a very, very deep sleep. For the first few seconds I had no idea where I was or what I was doing. Then suddenly, like a wave of consciousness washing over me, I remembered. I was in the X-Alps! I bounced out of bed full of energy and exuberance. Today I was on a mission.

With a big breakfast inside me, I set off from the van at 5am for the relatively short walk up to the take-off point above me. Once again the take-off wasn't obvious because the fields were very flat. Finally I found a spot on a gently sloping field. It was cross wind, but the wind was light, so with a good concerted run I was once again airborne skimming over the field and then out into the valley. It was a glorious feeling to be flying so early in the morning even if at the same time it felt slightly wrong. It felt like I was stealing the flight somehow from nowhere, paragliding isn't supposed to be like this, it's supposed to be about mid-afternoon flights in thermic air. Still my plan was working and with a katabatic flow of early morning air down the valley I was gliding at an impressive 12:1 in beautifully smooth air.

Nothing is easy in the X-Alps though and as I looked towards the end of the valley even my generous glide angle wasn't going to get me out of the valley. The valley turned north before connecting to the main valley, whereas I would need to go south. Still, this was not my most pressing concern. That was the high tension power lines in front of me. They ran along the length of the hillside I was flying along and I was about to be more or less level with them. The pylon in front of me however was the last pylon before the lines crossed the valley diagonally, dropping as they did so to the low hill in front separating this valley from the main valley. I quickly assessed the options. I could turn and fly parallel with the lines out into the valley. If I did this there were two possible scenarios, either the lines would be dropping steeper than my glide angle in which case I might be able to nip over them and continue or I'd have to double back and sneak under them against the pylon where they were at their highest. Neither option was great because I was already unlikely to make it out of the valley and the last part of the valley didn't look exactly full of landing options – either of these scenarios would mean losing more valuable height. As I pulled alongside the last pylon I realised that all I needed was some more height, glancing at the hillside there was a small steeply sloping field to my right just below the wires. With no time to lose I made a split-second decision, threw my weight over to the right and hauled on the inside brake. The glider banked hard propelling me directly at the slope, but rolled out just in time to deposit me, fly on the wall style, onto the field. It wasn't the prettiest landing but it did the job. I packed up the glider quickly and I set off up the hillside. With no path to follow I was climbing fences and wading through undergrowth, but I didn't need to go far. Gaining only a hundred meters of so I went under the power lines and found a nice big open field, with the grass freshly cut. For once it was steep enough to be a more typical launch spot, but high pine trees in front still meant I'd need all the height to clear them. Laying out at the highest point of the field I once again forward launched my glider, whooping my way over the tree tops (with only about a meter to spare!) and back out into the valley, now clear of the power lines. The extra height meant I could now head south west, over the small hill separating this valley from the main valley and it still left me plenty of height to cross the main valley and put some more kilometres behind me. The main valley was wide and full of big flat fields. It was also full of power lines going in every direction. It was crazy, there was not a single space with an 'easy' looking landing option. A large river and a main road also limited the options as I needed to end up on the correct side of these obstacles to avoid an unnecessary walk round to get back on track.

Finally I lined up for a field alongside the main road, sandwiched against the hillside. I packed up from my second flight of the day as normal people in the world were just finishing their breakfast and embarking on their commutes to the office. With the van just round the corner, I stopped for a second hearty breakfast and learnt that I'd just leapfrogged several places with those flights as most people in front of me had simply walked down that valley. This was the way to go. I was buoyed with success and eager to make the next move.

The day was supposed to get better, with potentially good flying weather due that afternoon. My plan was to get up on the south faces and work my way along the valley past Zell-am-See and then take the Gross-Glockner turn point on the west side. The leaders had already headed the more direct, but less flyable, route on the east side. It felt like an opportunity to catch up may come along, if I played my hand well. I headed for a hill above Goldegg, and found the most direct route took me through the town of Schwarzach. I always walked with a map and I was obsessed with taking the most efficient walking route on the ground. As I entered the town it looked like there was a route that went directly through a cluster of buildings. As I approached it there was a barrier across to stop traffic. I realised then that it was in fact a hospital. At exactly that moment my phone rang. It was my wife to say good morning. Instinctively she asked that innocuous of all questions, "where are you". Without thinking I replied, "In a hospital". Big mistake! Once the hysterics calmed down on the other end of the line I managed to explain that I was only walking through the hospital and was not in fact here for any treatment, the conversation went somewhat better!

As I started to ascend my second ascent of the day a lady came past on a bike. Obviously a fairly serious cyclist by the look of the bike she was riding, she slowed alongside me to say hello. She greeted me in English, clearly knowing who I was and what I was doing. After congratulating me she paused and then said in a motherly tone, "you have had breakfast haven't you", "yes!" I relied, "twice!" We both laughed and she carried on ahead of me.

Cutting the corners by walking across the fields to avoid the extra distance that the roads took around the hairpins, I began to realise that there were tracks through the dew laden grass, taking an almost identical route. This could only mean one thing – another X-Alps athlete had made the same choice. Sure enough, as I reached the point at which the tarmac of the road turned to gravel, the Spanish team's vehicle was parked up. Oriol Fernandez (ESP) was evidently in front of me. Oriol's supporter generously gave me a small bottle of water as I carried on up. Above me some morning cloud was beginning to thin. I had my eyes on a launchable slope just at the base of the cloud. Oriol had made a different choice – walking higher he was clearly intending to wait for the cloud to clear out. It was still quite early and my plan was simple, to fly over the col to the west, across a small gorge and land on the grassy slopes on the other side in order to walk up once again to a spot where I planned to start the 'real' flight of the day.

Aware that time was passing I quickly laid out the wing and, checking the lines carefully, turned to forward launch the wing. As I ran forwards the wing hung back, with one wing tip in particular feeling awkward and heavy. Glancing over my shoulder I saw immediately why the wing wasn't coming up. The lines had caught around a small root attached to a stump, which had then pulled the whole tree stump out the ground! I literally had a small tree stump hanging from my wing. It took a fair amount of detangling before I did finally manage to get off the hill properly. Once in the air there was some weak lifting air under the now dissipating clouds, but not enough to gain any height so I carried on, arriving in the col pretty low, but once again the wing carried me through. The problem was that the col was narrow and bent round to the right – I couldn't see what was on the other side until I was spat through the gap by the wind funnelling through it. In fact the ground flattened out with a few more fields before dropping away into the small gorge with the river and the road in the bottom. I really needed to cross the river in the air for this plan to work, so it was with my heart in my mouth that I skimmed over the last few trees before the slope dropped a hundred meters or so into the steep sided gorge.

That was the easy bit. The real challenge was that the nice big flat open fields on the other side were about 20m higher than I was going to arrive. What I was left with was a 45 degree tree covered slope dropping away to the river. There was just one open space on that slope, a steep rough looking patch of grass with a few cows in it. I swung the glider around in a perfect approach for my second fly-on-the-wall style landing of the day. About 30m from touching down, I realised that I was going to land bang in the middle of the space. Exactly the same place that the cows were! There was simply no other option, the gap and the approach were too tight. I realised that unless I did something I was literally about to land on a huge unsuspecting beast nonchalantly chewing the cud. I would definitely come off worse in such an encounter so I found myself shouting at the top of my voice for the cows to "MOOOVE". This spontaneous verbal explosion seemed to be the punch line to a joke that my six year old daughter would be proud of! The cows of course were startled and bolted just in time to clear my landing path.

The slope I'd put down on was indeed ridiculously steep and I had to use my hands to pull myself up and climb the fence at the top before popping out into the relative sanity of the open fields.

I began to realise I may have pushed it one flight too far – cumulus were replacing the inactive morning clouds and I had the distinct impression that I should be airborne soon in order to start a proper cross country flight. With a refilled camelback and some energy bars to munch on I again struck out up this next hill. As I did so both my Dad and I were making multiple calls, checking and reassessing the forecast. The information that was coming back was not great. Reports from the leader, Maurer, on the top of the Hochter pass were giving 70 km/h winds. Meanwhile the sky was beginning to look less attractive. The cumulus clouds were looking scraggier, rather than consolidating, and higher up the clouds were showing increasing signs of wave. This is caused when strong winds at altitude pass over big obstacles, like mountains, and set up a wave motion downwind. This can create some strange affects, apparently blocking the wind on the ground in places, whilst producing very dangerous winds in other areas as well as strong sink and turbulence. Having been caught in out-of-phase wave once before in the high mountains, I was cautious and advice coming back was that any cross-country flying was now looking increasingly less likely. Soon I was adjusting my intentions to just getting back into the air quickly in order to do yet another short hop. As I took a short cut straight up another ridiculously steep slope to where my father was waiting on a small single track road with the van, the TV helicopter came buzzing over my head filming me. Dad met me a few meters below the van and we quickly laid out the wing for yet another launch, barely being able communicate by shouting under the deafening noise from the rotor blades of the helicopter. My Dad told me that I "shouldn't muck this one up"! With a couple of bounds I was off down the valley. I soon noticed another glider ahead and slightly above me, which turned out to be Oriol, who had taken a different tactic to get to the same spot. I realised that with the good flying weather not materialising, there was only one option – the direct route to the Hochter pass. This meant crossing the valley and landing as close as I could to the route up towards Rauris. Spotting a field and some tracks leading up through the trees, I crossed the valley and put the wing down in what was a much more sedate landing. A quick study of the map and my situation was even better than I had thought. Instead of going up through the forest, I could traverse round on a small farm track. This would take me into the gorge where the map showed a footpath following the river up into the valley I needed to follow. With this choice I'd leave Oriol behind, who'd continued gliding along the valley heading west.

As my farm track connected to the footpath I was surprised to see a wide and very well-trodden route. As I set of along it there were also more people than I'd been expecting. Through a small tunnel in the rock and out onto a suspended walkway I soon realised that my direct route was in fact along one of those well-advertised tourist routes, allowing people to see spectacular gorges and waterfalls on a short scenic walk. This was just amazing, the gorge was indeed stunning and the path criss-crossed it in a series of spectacular bridges and walkways. I enjoyed this very much, except for one major drawback. It was absolutely full to choking point with tourists and they were all going extremely slowly. I was told to slow down several times by disgruntled Austrians (ok, I admit, I do understand some German!) and I found myself fuming behind overweight people unable to negotiate even the simplest of steps at anything more than crawling pace.

Luckily for me the 'pretty bit' was mercifully short and most people clearly turned and descended as soon as they'd seen the gorge, so once I was above that part I had the path more or less to myself once again.

Emerging onto the main road I finally decided to rest. It was lunch time, my feet deserved a soak, and I needed a proper refuel. I'd come a long way in a morning, I was pretty proud of myself as most of it had been done in the air despite the lack of thermals to aid me on my journey. However, the rest of my afternoon was clear – there was nothing else to do except walk the long valley to the Hochter pass.

With fine weather and wind at altitude reassuring me that no one would be flying over my head, I continued on my way at a brisk pace. The only remarkable event on that long and stunningly beautiful walk was my cut through the town of Rauris. I figured the town centre was a little shorter than the main road and in any case I needed the toilet and the thought of a proper toilet to sit on and empty my bowels was really quite attractive even after only 3 days of 'roughing it'. The trouble was, as I walked through the town there was no evidence of a public toilet anywhere. I wasn't prepared to put in any significant deviation from my route but at the same time I was getting more and more in need. Amongst the last few shops in the town was an Intersport and there in the window was the manager modifying his display. Seeing me coming down the road in my X-Alps T-shirt he quickly jumped down and met me on the pavement. He was full of questions, but I didn't let him get through many of his before I interjected with my own. "Do you have a toilet I can use?" It was the simplest thing, but it was an absolute luxury, a clean toilet, a wash basin and a soft fluffy towel. I felt like all my Christmases had come at once.

Onwards and upwards. The road and path slowly rose through this valley heading towards the Hochter pass. Soon the road became a track and before long I was arriving at the road head. The weather had forced the whole field through this way so there was a constant stream of athletes coming through here. This also meant the race media were here in force. After many hours walking in the heat I finally stopped to rest at this last parking before the track turned into a steep trail. Another change of shoes and a refuel was in order. I drank a mixing bowl full of soup and ate goodness knows what else before restocking with energy bars for the push up to over 2500m. I set off at pace, determined to catch the athletes who I knew were not far in front of me – Mike Kung and Thomas De

Dorlodot (BEL). For the first section I had the TV cameraman keeping pace with me (in fact, he was like a puppy dog, running off in front and then finding a spot to film me from before catching me up again, walking with me for a while and then repeating the whole exercise!). I rather enjoyed his company – simply having someone to talk to whilst walking took my mind off the fact I'd been on the go for over 12 hours, virtually non-stop. As we came round a curve in the track together I spotted a herd of cows next to the road and joked he had a chance to get the classic cow shot (having cows in the foreground of these types of photos seems to be rather sought after!). I was in fact only joking but on seeing the cows he sprinted off ahead of me, leapt the fence and dived into the field to try to get the perfect footage, alas he was too late and I was not prepared to slow down.

I left my friendly cameraman behind and passed the last building before the path became really steep. It was a little mountain lodge with a couple outside being served beer by the waiter. As I stopped a few meters away at a trough to fill up my water container, I overheard the waiter explaining to the walkers what I was up to. They listened to him with incredulity. No time to stop and bask in their amazement though, I still wanted to catch Mike. After half an hour or so I came round a corner and there I could see the path curving steeply upwards to my left and the unmistakable figure of an X-Alps athlete making his way surprisingly slowly up the path. Another half an hour and I caught him, but it was Thomas, not Mike. Apparently Mike had passed Thomas some time earlier at "almost a run". I'd been going a lot quicker than Thomas but I'd also quickened my pace to catch him up, so I was happy to slow a little and at the same time he was motivated to speed up a little to stay with me. So for the first time on the race I found myself walking with a fellow competitor. Mentally we pulled each other up that hill. It was a tough ascent. Because of my short flights I'd only walked up hills today, so I had basically been walking uphill non-stop since before dawn. Those early flights felt like a long, long time ago now.

The path here joins the famous Gross Glockner road which snakes its way over the high mountains. At this point it dives through a short tunnel into the valley on the other side. We were not allowed to use the tunnel. The rules state that any tunnel connecting two valley systems is prohibited, so we had the pleasure of another 100m vertically to ascend before we were over the top. We paused just before the top to take some pictures of each other. 'Just before' the top was important, the wind was howling on the other side, as we walked the last few meters over the ridge we were hit by the full force of the wind. It was icy cold cutting straight through our sweat soaked clothes and stinging our cheeks. My head was bowed against the wind going downhill, the going should have been easier but my legs hurt with every step down the steep path. Soon I was dressed in my winter down jacket with an outer layer to keep off the wind. I was wearing my hat and mountaineering gloves to walk in and only just staying warm enough.

Despite the wind we did see a glider in the air, and high in front of us. It was Jouni Makkinon (FIN) the Finnish competitor. I'd been here in similar conditions in training and I knew there was a convergence zone out in the main valley – Jouni's presence proved this was the case again, we just had to get down the mountain far enough to be able to launch safely. Finding a spot to launch I got the glider out. Although I knew flying was the right thing to do here, I felt tired, nervous of the conditions and generally a little unsure of myself. This showed in the fact that it took me three attempts to get off the hill.

The wind picked me up off the ground vertically, straight up and away from the hill. I lifted my legs and hooked the speed bar inside my pod harness. I relaxed as my forward speed was fine – double digits even! As I moved further out the speed got better and the lift increased – the valley convergence area was working. Still, I knew this convergence was localised and that there was a lot of wind around at this level (I was already above the height of the pass I'd just walked over where it had been so windy I'd barely been able to stand!) so I decided not to try to maximise my height but instead get the turn point as quickly as I could. Unlike the Dachstein where we had to pass through a fixed gate on the glacier this 'turn point' consisted of a 6km cylinder centred on the Gross Glockner peak itself. From the direction I was approaching this meant I just had to fly about 2km along the valley towards the peak. The road clung to the mountainside here, taking tourists up to the observation area at the foot of the main glacier. As I headed down this valley I left the convergence and at the same time my groundspeed accelerated alarmingly. With no lift now, I was down to the level of the road. As my groundspeed went past 70 km/h I was just thankful that the mountainside was exposed and grassy. As I approached the turn point things started to get very scary indeed. The valley was funnelling down into a narrow gap and my instruments told me I still had 200m left to get the turn point. I realised that this meant I'd need to fly round a spur. Despite the fact I was so close I knew carrying on would be suicidal. The wind was now around 40km/h and would be faster through the gap as I was getting lower and the valley was coming up to meet me. There would be severe turbulence behind the spur and even if I did make it there, there would be no way I'd get back against that wind low in the gully. I had no choice but to swing the glider round into wind and slope land below the road.

Speed packing at the Gross Glockner turn point.
Photo: Chris Hoerner/Red Bull Content Pool

I packed quickly as time was against me. I was joined by another TV cameraman (this time from a Russian film crew) and a cow who decided my glider was very interesting. So they got a cow shot in the end! As soon as the wing was in the bag I ran, still wearing all my flying clothes, for the road and then along the road to the turn point. I was holding my flying instruments in front of me and soon the little jingle played telling me I'd made the turn point. I turned and ran with all my strength down the road back towards the convergence area and the lighter wind. The problem was it was already 8.30pm and we were not allowed to be in the air after 9pm. Being stuck up on the mountain would not be ideal – I needed to get back into the air and fly down to the valley floor. After a kilometre I knew it would be ok here, so I threw my wing out below the road and quickly clipped in to launch again.

Hasty launch as time is running out.
Photo: Chris Hoerner/Red Bull Content Pool

The wind was across the slope but I wasn't too concerned. I pulled the wing up and it came up nicely, but I slipped so I tried to control the wing with the right brake line. Nothing, the brake line was locked, I pulled it and nothing happened. Everything seemed to speed up, I was going down the slope barely off the ground, with no control of the wing. Somehow I was in the air but I was sinking fast and I had no control with my right hand. As the ground thankfully began to drop away I swung the glider round to face down the valley and take a look at the brake line. Somehow the brake handle had gone through a loop of brake line below the pulley and was completely locked. I pulled a little brake line in and tried to untangle it, but I could only do this by leaning to the right and pulling on the brake line, this of course started to induce a hard turn to the right. I was in a precarious situation with precious little height to play with so I decided I'd just steer by holding the line above the pulley and concentrate on flying my way out of here. The valley I was in was actually quite high up and dropped very steeply about a kilometre further on, where the convergence started. The problem was that I was not yet in the convergence and I was against the wind here. With the road now lost high above me I realised I was in pretty strong sink still so I pushed the bar. Groundspeed was ok, but I was beginning to look at the trees below trying to identify landable clearings as I still wasn't sure I'd make it out. Finally my groundspeed increased and the vario indicated the air was no longer sinking. Soon it was beeping away merrily – I'd made it back to the convergence, only just though. If I was physically tired, I was mentally a wreck. I still had a locked out brake line, I was in the air with only about 15mins to the land by time, in strong convergence (I was flying in a straight line going up at about 1.8m/s) and it was still extremely windy. Even in the convergence there was quite a bit of head wind, I was now over a 1000m above the ground as the valley floor had dropped away. Irrationally I started to panic that I wasn't going to make it back to the ground in time. The convergence seemed to have no end, so I pushed the speed bar trying to get distance from the height. I decided this was not enough so I put in 'big ears' as well. I still had my sunglasses on but with a completely overcast sky the light was fading fast. It seemed like even nature was trying to remind me that my time was nearly up. I could barely see in the valley below me and so I had to take off my glasses. Being too scared to let go of the controls long enough to stow them properly, I held them between my teeth for the rest of the flight!

It was only now that I was out of the convergence and certain to make the ground on time that I noticed Thomas just above me. He'd walked down even further from where I'd launched to find a better spot and had then taken more height in the convergence which had allowed him to get the turn point in the air with considerably more height than me (meaning he wasn't down in the gulley where I was). He'd flown over the top of me as I launched for the second time. Later he told me that my launch looked 'pretty scary from above'. I guess it was, because it was terrifying from where I had been! As we both flew down the valley in the fading evening light I looked at the landing options – there were plenty of fields but obstacles were difficult to spot in this light. I knew there was a cable strung across the valley at some point here so I decided for once not to try to stretch the glide. I'd been lucky today so far and I did not want to ruin it now. I also still had limited control as it had proved impossible to untangle the brake line in flight. I finished the flight with a few wide turns and a comfortable landing in a big field. I looked back at the imposing mountains around me and I couldn't help feeling I'd only just escaped their clutches tonight. I packed up and set off walking down the valley. Thomas had landed in front of me but I guess I was a little quicker packing as we were soon walking together again comparing experiences in what was now the pitch black.

Meeting up with my Dad again for a huge dinner, he told me he'd spoken to the Russian film crew who'd probably spent a pretty cold day standing around up on the mountain and only seen a few gliders from a distance. They had remarked to my Dad, after my somewhat frenetic run followed by me falling off the side of the mountain under my glider, that 'that was quite exciting wasn't it?'

I walked in the dark until 11pm. The walk was punctuated by being stopped by the police who'd been informed that there had been a paragliding accident involving one of the X-Alps pilots. Fortunately we were all safe and well, but I could quite understand any onlooker with a knowledge of paragliding thinking that any of the aerial events in the area that day had resulted in an accident. In order to put them at ease I called the race director and gave the police my phone so they could check with the race organisers. I of course continued walking but began to get a little worried after 15mins when the police car was no longer in sight and I did not have my phone, still if you can't trust the police who can you trust! Sure enough they returned the phone to me. Shortly afterwards a TV film crew came along in an estate car with the camera man sat in the back with the tailgate open. These guys drove in front of me for about 30mins while they filmed my late night walk. Despite

becoming a little tired of having a camera in my face all the
time, this one was welcome, because it meant I was much safer
than walking along this fast road alone with only a head torch
to alert oncoming traffic. All the time they were filming I was
on the phone, first to Tom to check forecast and strategy for
the next day, then to my wife and then finally to my father as it
was now quarter to 11 and the rules stated we had to stop at
11pm. He assured me that he was in range and I'd get to him
by 11pm. With five minutes to go I passed the Belgians spot
for the night and became more worried. Another call and he
reassured me he was just around the corner. Luckily he was. I
made it to the van at 10.59. What a day. With six small flights
and continuing to push, I'd managed to get myself back into
the top 10. Furthermore there were a few pilots around me
who had just been given penalties for infringements of Salzburg
airspace on the first day. They'd have to sit out the next day. I
was heading back up the rankings!

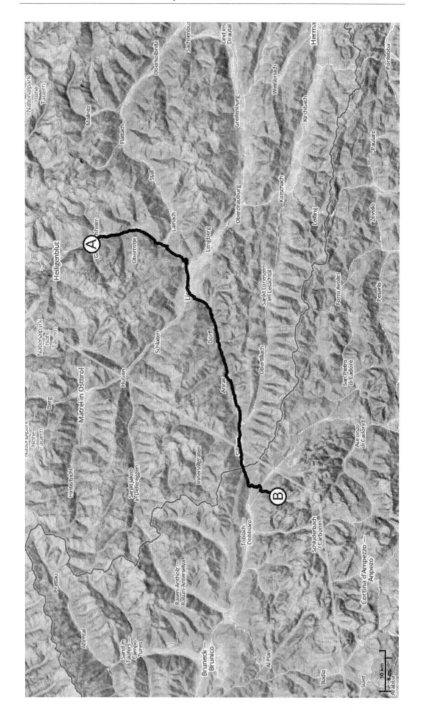

Day 4: Grosskirchheim to the foot of Tre Cime

On days when it is possible to fly, no matter how small those opportunities are, this race is amazing. Day 3 had been a blast, tough for sure, as I'd pushed hard, but I'd got myself where I wanted to be. Now I needed to consolidate that, and the weather was not forecast to be good. Rain with a brighter spell around lunch, but always with some wind high up, meant it wasn't a forgone conclusion that we wouldn't fly, but it stacked the odds against us. As I'd headed south from the Gross Glockner following the ground route, most of the 'chasing gaggle' just in front had taken a more direct, and more mountainous line. This difference in route would prove to work in my favour, but it certainly was not a tactical decision. The group in front, flying the same convergence zone I had the day before, had been able to push through a high pass to Kals. Maurer, now the clear race leader had managed to fly despite the strong wind as far as the foot of the Tre Cime in the Dolomites. An incredible flight given how extreme the conditions were. No one else in that pack had been able to take advantage of these strong conditions and were mostly in and around Kals. The reason I had not followed in that route was simply that time didn't allow – I only just had enough time to make it to the valley floor in my last flight. Jouni, whom I'd seen high as I'd crossed the Hochter pass had not managed to reconnect with the road network or his supporter and had spent a night out in the back of beyond. I'd probably been about an hour later into the air than he was so there had been no chance of me taking that route.

The valley route, south to Winkeln and then over a low pass to Lienz before heading due west along the valley, was not as direct but was about as flat as you can get in the big mountains. As it was still not clear if it would be possible to fly or not the optimal route wasn't clear at this point. Even if only a flight down was possible the group who'd taken the direct route could hike up the north faces of the massif in front of them and then glide down to the valley I'd be heading up, undoubtedly in front of me. Without any flying opportunities the flat way would be more efficient, but the deck was already set – fate had this time made my choice for me. For once I was hoping that it was not flyable, despite not looking forward to a long trudge.

I'd started walking late – sometime after 5am. Thomas, who'd spent the night a little further back had characteristically set off closer to 4am (the earliest allowed). Still, I was in good form and walking fast. By the time I was in Winkeln the rain was coming down hard. I'd already had two food stops but it was only mid-morning. The road made just 2 hairpins as it ascended this pass. As normal, I had my detailed walking map strung around my neck in an old fashioned map case and I could see a foot path that allowed me to cut both these switch backs. I cut through some houses on the outskirts of the town and popped out to cross the main road onto the direct footpath. As I did so I saw for the first time that day Thomas walking away from me about 200m up the road with an umbrella. He'd missed the short cut which I would have happily shown him, but he was too far away to hear my shout. Although I was walking faster than Thomas (I'd set of nearly an hour after him, after all) this didn't really matter too much in the grand scheme of things. One day someone can walk maybe 5km further, but as soon as you are flying that difference is insignificant. What is much more important in this race is to get in a good position for the flying weather when it comes. At this stage of the game a difference of a couple of kilometres separating 5th and 6th place is irrelevant. Knowing all that didn't stop me feeling a little smug at catching him up though!

Half way up the footpath I had called my Dad and 'ordered' scrambled eggs and sausage and a cup of hot tea to be ready at the pass (how British!). It was only just as I was polishing off the last of the sausage and eggs and downing the tea that the Belgian team vehicle pulled in behind ours and a bedraggled Thomas appeared, walking up the road. I repressed any outward signs of smugness as we discussed together the next step.

A couple of hours in front of us, Ferdinand Van Shelven (NED), the unknown Dutchman had come this same way and flown down to Lienz. Looking at the competition before the race, I'd unreasonably written off Ferdy as an 'also ran'. He had been anything but in the first few days of the race and little did I know it then, but he would continue to be one of the men to match during much of the race.

As the road passed over the col there was a track off to the right and it is from here that Ferdy had launched. Thomas and I were discussing this option, I was still sitting in the van and he was at the door with full waterproof gear in the steady rain. There was little wind here as is typical with such sustained rain, the problem was indeed only the rain. Thomas assured me his brother had already driven round the corner to the take-off and the 'rain was lighter there, only little drops'. I looked at the water streaming down the windscreen. I was unconvinced.

The problem with flying paragliders in the rain is that the fabric becomes heavier when wet and water can accumulate inside them, performance is deteriorated and if there is a collapse or other issue the material is likely to stick to itself preventing reopening. Typically the stall speed will be higher and the wing will be more difficult to launch. Not a great idea then, but also not a show stopper if you are in the X-Alps. Irrespective of the fact that the wing performs less well it also needs to be considered that once packed away wet it will mostly likely weigh around a kilo more in the bag. That is a big deal.

What we were considering was a 'top-to-bottom' flight of no more than about 600m. The take-off was not on route and the additional detour plus the unpacking and repacking time meant in this case the benefit was actually quite marginal. Waiting 15mins for a heavy period of rain to pass for example could be enough to make the whole thing no longer worthwhile. The final factor at play here was saving our legs. Irrespective of time this would save some of the hammering descending the other side would exert on our knees.

As we walked along the road together we weighed up these options and finally made our own choices. Thomas would fly down in the rain, whilst I'd walk. At the junction we said good bye and wished each other good luck.

As usual I was in short cut finding mode and descended these low slopes through trees, fields and houses mainly on footpaths. About a third of the way down I saw Thomas fly past to the north of me. The rain was still persistent. He recorded a video diary of that flight which clearly shows how hard it was raining. Seeing him only made me accelerate, bounding down the hill and at one point taking a short cut across fields, ensuring my damp feet were now soaked through by the long grass. A little more than half way down the rain eased and by the valley floor it had more or less stopped. I cursed, but I couldn't have known it would stop at that point and depending on how quick Thomas had packed he was probably only a kilometre or so in front of me in any case.

A quick stop in Lienz for dry shoes and socks and it was time to start pushing up the valley. I stopped for lunch in the same lay-by as Thomas, so finally our different choices made little difference, although I was happy my glider was still dry!

The dry period had developed into a more sustained sunny spell and all focus was now on how flyable the day was. Things started to get interesting as Ferdy, some way in front, was starting to head up the mountain side instead of continuing along the valley. At the same time, behind me, Heli had launched from the same place as Thomas had and was now circling and climbing above Lienz. With texts arriving with this info I needed to analyse what was going on. Whilst spectators on live tracking assumed Heli was thermalling, it was clear to me he was climbing in convergence. This was because the wind in the valley I was now walking up was blowing consistently down the valley. Although the sun was now out, there clearly were not many thermals around as otherwise the wind would be coming up the valley. Armed with this information, I decided walking up the side of the mountain, as Ferdy was doing, would be futile as I'd be unlikely to climb and I would make very little progress within the valley against the wind in any case. Reluctantly my instincts told me to keep walking. They were right.

Fortunately there was a cycle path that followed the south side of the river which made the long walk much more tolerable by keeping me off the main road on the other side of the river. Taking only short breaks for food and refills of my drinking system, I continued like this through the afternoon. As I approached the town of Sillian in the late afternoon I had the unexpected offer of a shower at Blue Sky Paragliding. Taking them up on the chance, I stopped off there to find a whole group of pilots, unable to fly because of the wind, glued to a TV screen showing the live tracking of the race. They were a little surprised when I showed no interest in checking this in passing. I was only focussed on an efficient pit stop. As I showered, my Dad prepared dinner and once clean again I wolfed down a huge plate of food in front of the Paragliding school's dog who sat expectantly at the van door eyeing my plate in hope. I denied him any of the food, finishing every scrap.

This stopping point, which many pilots took advantage of, also turned out to be the point where the two groups of athletes came back together. Last night I was at the back of this lot and now I was near the front, but very little still separated us all.

I had talked to the local pilots about walking up about 2000m to the ridge that separated Austria from the Dolomites and flying onto the Tre Cime mountain range from there. Looking at the ridge the clouds were moving fast over it and betting on the wind dropping seemed foolish as walking round was not such a big deal. Once again I reluctantly admitted that walking was the best option. Setting off I somehow managed to leave with the van key. I'm sure my Dad really appreciated the sprint he had to do to catch me up, some way away already!

Italy at last! Hiking near Vierschach.
Photo: Felix Woelk/Red Bull Content Pool

As the race progressed I became more and more amazed at how many people were following our progress live online. As I passed some apartment buildings leaving the town, some people hung out of their windows shouting my name, waving excitedly and taking pictures.

Next stop was Italy and I crossed the border on a small footpath on the opposite side of the river to the main road. A new country and not even the opportunity to take a picture of an 'Italy' road sign to prove it. It was really quite a pleasant evening now and the final push for the remaining hours would take me over a spur in the forest. Once again I seemed surrounded by photographers as I set off up through the forestry tracks. My direct route approach soon led me to cut directly up though the forest crossing and re-crossing the forestry track. I caught a glimpse of the Belgian support vehicle (one of the few teams using a 4 wheel drive) zipping up through the forest, checking out the route. Thomas wouldn't be all that far behind. With the light fading fast I came out of the forest to see the path down taking me in a different direction than I needed to go. I could see my father below me waiting with the van. I took a direct line, straight over open fields to him. It was getting late and the last leg was steeply uphill to the road head on the way up to Tre Cime. By 10.30pm I was exhausted. The road head was the right target but I honestly wanted nothing else but just to stop, particularly when the road became really steep. I pushed on and made it to the car park. The Dutch team's motor-home was there. I'd caught Ferdy up. Yes!

After some 82 kilometres of walking (and the second longest distance on foot of any of the athletes that day) I'd not only consolidated my gains of day 3, I built on them. I was now officially one to watch according to the race reports. I went to bed exhausted, happy and entirely convinced that my legs would never work again.

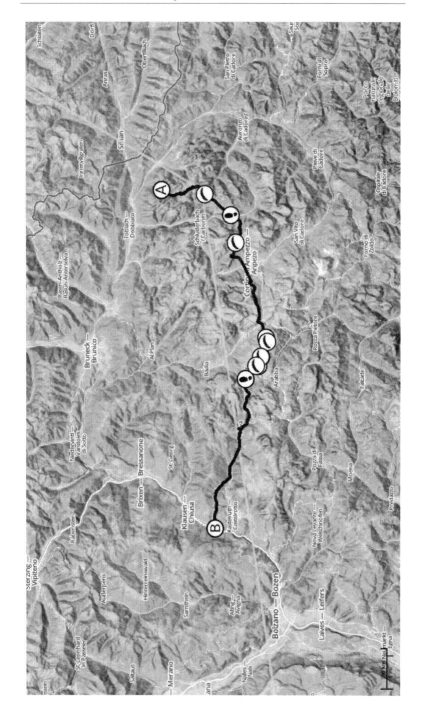

Day 5: Tre Cime to Waidbruck

Concerned for a way to ensure my legs would indeed survive the onslaught of repeatedly covering huge distances by foot my father had found a cooling gel. He'd been trying to buy some 'instant ice' packs but, unable to find them, he'd bought this instead. It turned out to have both a cooling effect as well as being stuffed full of arnica. Up to this point I'd always shunned arnica as something reserved for my children's bumps and bruises. Irrationally I had thought that real men didn't need arnica. In fact it was the perfect remedy to provide soothing relief to my leg muscles and I'd gratefully smothered it all over my legs the night before. That morning, as I set off in the darkness, I realised my legs felt wonderful. Rightly or wrongly, I put this down to the new gel and accordingly named it 'magic cream'. This magic cream, along with various foot creams, now became an integral part of my evening ritual to keep my body in shape.

The truth was, much to my surprise, I felt absolutely on top of the world. The weather forecast was good for the day and as the first light crept into the sky there was not a cloud to be seen. This walk, up the north side of the Tre Cime, was one of the most breathtaking moments of the whole adventure. I paused to take numerous photos and videos as I climbed up in the shade with the early morning sun lighting up the ethereal peaks above me. There was a dusting of snow on the higher summits from the rain yesterday that had fallen as snow at altitude. With no phone signal here, I really was alone. For once even the thousands of people following me online could not see what I was up to. My thoughts turned to the real world, of people starting to rise from their beds soon to head to work for the day. With that thought in my head I sincerely wished I could teleport everyone following online to this place at this moment. I wanted to share it with the world, but somehow no photo or video would do it justice.

My euphoria continued as I approached the Tre Cime hut at 2400m and bumped into Ferdy along with his supporter who had walked up with him. We walked the flat section together crossing the col to the East of the main peak and remarking on the frost on the path. Ferdy had been setting off from his van just as I had hauled myself out of bed – I'd stuck my head out of the door to say 'hi'. The fact that I'd caught him on the walk up, despite having set off some 30minutes later fed my confidence further. I was pushing hard because I had what I thought was a smart plan, but was to turn out to be the first in an almost catastrophic chain of errors.

As we came over the high point, I left Ferdy behind as he stopped to reshuffle things from his supporters bag to his own as his supporter headed back down to the van. The high point seemed much more than just a watershed, it was more like the division between two different worlds. Behind me the solitary and serenely beautiful world occupied only by privileged competitors in the world's most extreme race, in front there were swarms of day trippers, cagoule-wearing walkers and general tourists having paid the exorbitant fee to drive the toll road that came up this south face of the Tre Cime. I pressed on, bounding past the sightseers, time was ticking and I wanted to get an early flight off this mountain to start my cross country flight further to the west. There was a headwind forecast but as I came round onto the west face there was virtually no wind at all, so I laid the wing out on an extremely rocky slope. Just about ready to launch Ferdy arrived and took a look at the situation. Unknown to me at the time we were now in 4th and 5th position having passed a couple of others in this area.

It was about 8.40am as I forward launched. The glide down to Misurata looked marginal but I was sure I'd make it out over the trees. My plan was to walk over the Tre Coci Col and start my cross country flight on the south faces further on. I thought I had plenty of time, and was surprised to find myself flying through buoyant, even lifting, air in places. Out in the valley the wind was blowing lightly from the north, pushing me in the direction I needed to go and I assumed, wrongly, the lift was simply the patchy dynamic lift created by this valley wind. With hindsight it was the first stirrings of the days thermals. If I'd realised that at the time I'd have worked them for all I could to stay airborne, but I was too fixated on my plan. With the lift and the tailwind I made it past Misurata, but without enough height to get over the tree covered col. I landed at the side of the main road and left some clothing I didn't need tied to a fence post for my Dad to pick up.

As I packed I saw the first puffs of cumulus appearing. Now I needed to shift. I strode up to the top of the col as fast as I could. My target was the south faces where Paul Guschlbauer, the young and incredibly talented Austrian, was waiting to launch in third place. Excitement reigned amongst people following my race 'wow, you are only 1 km behind a podium place', they wrote on my guestbook. The problem was I did not share their confidence, I knew I should be getting ready to take off not pushing hard up a mountainside. Nevertheless it was all still to play for.

The path headed up a ski slope which snaked its way behind the south facing cliffs I wanted to fly. I was worried this slope would be in the lee and didn't even stop to look whether it was a launchable option. Instead I continued across to the top of a cliff. The take-off options were not good. A gully looked too dangerous with not enough space to launch properly. On a high point there was a bonfire built on a flat space, with a short steep slope in front at about 45 degrees before it dropped away to the cliff below. As I arrived there was a light but steady breeze, enough I figured to get off here. I cleared a little of the debris from the bonfire and laid out the wing. There really wasn't enough space and alarm bells should have already been ringing, but I was impatient having already seen one of my fellow competitors, perhaps Ferdy, coming round the cliffs from the direction of Tre Cime at cloud base and passing me. With my Dad holding the wing up to the now non-existent air flow, and me teetering on the point where the flat ground dropped away at about 45 degrees, I hauled on the wing. It didn't come up properly and I quickly put it back down, picking myself out of the bushes I'd fallen into from the few steps I'd had to take backwards.

I was so focussed on getting into the air, I was not thinking straight. If I had have been I'd have paused and reassessed the situation. Instead I tried the same thing a second time, convinced that if I brought the wing up with a strong enough pull I could power myself off the cliff backwards. It was madness. I hauled on the risers and pulled the wing, this time it was above my head as I disappeared backwards over the edge.

The last thing I saw was the wing above me but not properly inflated with the tips collapsed then I saw bushes, heard branches breaking and I knew my fate was out of my hands. When everything stopped moving I realised I was hanging across the slope above the very last bit of sloping ground, right on the edge of a sheer cliff. If I looked over my left side there was nothing for about 100m vertically. The wing was tangled round some big bushes with lines coming down to my harness from both sides. Dad was already trying to sort the mess out on the far side, but I had to shout to him to stop.

For all my impatience of a few moments before, I was now mentally in a different place. The day was forgotten, the race was forgotten, nothing else mattered but getting out of this predicament in one piece. As I was able to get my feet onto the ground, I could stand up but the slope was covered in loose rock and was far too steep to balance on without a hand hold. Luckily the bushes were strong and I hauled my way through a small gap in the bushes, still in my harness, bringing as much of the lines as I could with me. Finally I got myself out at the top and stepped out of the harness and threw off my warm flying clothes. The day was scorching hot and we had a job to do.

If falling off a cliff wasn't already dangerous enough, what we then did was insane. We climbed back down, one of us on each side of the big bushes, and started, line by line, picking the glider out. All the time we were hanging on to the bushes with one hand whilst stretching as far out as we could to unpick lines. One slip from either of us and we'd have been dead at the bottom of the cliff. We worked carefully and methodically, all the time imploring each other to be careful. I only became really worried when my Dad remarked that he 'hoped this pallet is properly jammed'. Asking for clarification he informed me that a pallet from the makeshift bonfire had obviously slipped over the edge on his side and it was this, and only this, that he was reliant on clambering up and down to the lines. Images of the pallet becoming dislodged and sliding down the mountain filled me with horror, but we carried on.

The quiet calm that had come over me remained. I thought my day, if not my race was basically over with this mistake. As my Dad showed me the frayed end of a line I was now convinced I had an unflyable wing. Finally after about 30mins we pulled the wing out and spent some time on the top in a flat grassy clearing checking the wing and the lines. Bizarrely we could not find the broken line. Modern paragliders do not have all that many lines, and so it should not have been difficult to find, but I for one began to doubt its existence. This was crazy we'd both seen the frayed end…

So what to do? I figured if the line was an upper line then chances were I could still fly it and fix it later. Otherwise

I'd need to walk back down to the car to get the repair kit, or wait for Dad to do this, either way that would take about an hour and a half.

We needed to find somewhere to pull the glider up and if all being well, launch finally. Dad went back up to the bonfire and said optimistically that there was now a breeze there. Too dangerous, I said. I figured having narrowly escaped death it was not advisable to see if I could get away with it one more time. Looking round for other options I made my way back to the grassy ski slope that the path had come up. Despite being slightly behind the cliff, the wind was flowing smoothly up this gap and the take-off was wide and pleasant. What on earth had I been doing faffing around on top of that cliff for?! Fortunately for me the broken line did turn out to be an upper, inner, c-line, meaning flying without it was possible. So about an hour later than should have been the case, and now with many pilots having passed me, I was back in the air and covering the kilometres once again.

Although there was lifting air around there were no strong climbs in the area I'd launched into. I had two choices. Either I could back track to the pass where a mass of cloud indicated strong lift or head along route – flying along a knife edge spine of rock. I opted for the later, eager to get the kilometres under me, but the first section was devoid of lifting air and I was soon skimming the rocky cliffs. I had to get a climb here as the next part involved me crossing the Cortina valley. I need not have worried; soon I was screaming skywards in a powerful climb, despite there being no cloud above me. Once high I set off across the valley. There was now quite a lot of cloud around and I flew towards the east face of the mountains above Cortina. I really needed to be on the south face, but a spine blocked my route and worryingly the whole of the south and east faces were in shade. I had to tell myself to be patient as I approached this area, despite the fact that every instinct in me was wanting to race, to make up for my mistakes.

As I arrived, I joined a weak climb and relaxed, it was enough to get me over the spine to a stronger thermal and before long I was soaring up alongside the vertical rock walls of the mighty Dolomites. As I climbed a whole new world opened up in front of me, mountain huts and rocky landscapes which had been hidden from view to everyone below, now came into sight. I was now cruising around wispy bits of cloud at over 3000m and moving quickly heading west and out of the Dolomites.

I still felt uneasy. I'd never flown in the Dolomites before and as I came to the top cable car station above the Falzarego pass I was hit by indecision. The situation was certainly impressive and crowds of people lined the cliff top walks enjoying the summer sunshine. As I came in level with the top (to the cheers and waves of the spectators) I realised there would be no climbs here, it was buoyant with air rising off the cliffs, but there were no thermals being triggered. I was flying alongside a blue glider, not a competitor, and he headed north round the cliffs. In my tiredness I followed him before realising that was not the route I'd planned and not the route I needed to follow. I needed to keep heading west here, over another north-south ridge to my west and then hopefully over the Gardena pass and out of the Dolomites. There was a large cloud just to the south, which, I figured, was the reason there were no climbs on the cliff itself. The area was confusing, a sort of 3 way pass, but this large black cloud sucking strongly seemed to make sense to me. Based on this knowledge I headed first south with a plan to then turn west to make it over the ridge. It was a good theory. It was also wrong!

As I headed out from the cliff and under the overdeveloping cloud, I was sinking fast. Clearly the cloud wasn't working so I turned west, still confident that I'd now pass along the south end of the ridge in order to get onto the west face. Fate had other ideas though. I flew through strongly sinking air going from nearly 3000m to the deck in what seemed like no time. Despite flying the wing as fast as I could I simply couldn't escape the sink. I didn't make it over the north-south ridge, instead ending up on the shallow easterly slopes at the south end. All was not lost though, I was only just below the grassy spine that blocked my route onto the west face. After unsuccessfully flirting with an extremely weak patch of lifting air, I landed the wing on this high grassy slope. Hanging on for longer would have meant sinking below the tree line, and then I'd have been in the valley bottom on the wrong side of the mountain. I preferred to land and preserve my altitude.

I was so close to the ridge that I didn't even pack the wing up, I just bundled it up and walked in my harness, still dressed in full flying gear. What had looked like a few minutes walk turned out to be rather more and by the time I came over the ridge I was hot, sweaty and exhausted. The sky was over-developing fast and I was surprised to find no breeze at all on this face. I weighed up my options. Looking north along the ridge, a small cliff extended about 200m above me and several kilometres into the distance. I was level with the bottom of this cliff, but the slopes were very shallow off to the west. I could walk up above the cliffs and be in a better position to climb away in what thermals were now left in this greying sky, or launch here and risk sinking out. If I had my glider in the rucksack I may have made a different decision but I didn't. I was getting frustrated and annoyed with the situation, everything seemed to be going wrong and just to remind me of my errors, two X-Alps competitors flew over my head and climbed away in a weak climb from the cliffs above me. I could have screamed with frustration.

With a few intrepid walkers stopping to watch, I forward launched off the shallow hillside and set off north. I never even connected with the base of the cliff, instead sinking down the shallow slopes. At one point a patch of open ground on a particularly shallow part presented itself as an obstacle. I could either turn away from the slope and fly out and around, losing more precious height, or I could land there. I touched down here but instead of dropping the glider, I leant forwards, weight on the risers and ran about 40m across the hillside to where the slope dropped away a bit more and I was back airborne. My ambitions were now reduced to simply getting off this hillside now and getting at least down to the town or Corvara. As I tracked left, the ground below rose up to a low pass in front of me. I couldn't really see the pass properly but it was clear I wasn't going to make it over, so once again I slope landed. This time, I packed the glider quickly and set off walking up the hill.

After about 100m two things happened at the same time. The unmistakable wing of Guschlbauer launched above me from the top of the cliffs. It turned out he had made a similar mistake to me, getting drilled and landing in the valley behind this ridge, although unlike me had not compounded his error with impatience and had instead hiked to a good launch spot. The second thing was a nice breeze blowing steadily up the hillside – unmistakably a thermal. I watched as Paul flew delicately out from the ridge, clearly with little lift under the grey sky until he was above me and climbed away, slowly but surely, in the very thermal I was feeling drawing the air up the slope.

Quickly, I threw out the wing; I was on a steep part of the hill and should be able to climb from here. I quickly laid out the glider, expecting a reverse launch even. But, by the time I was clipped in there was not a breath of wind. I screamed out loud in frustration. As I stood there facing my wing and watching Paul now flying off in the direction of the Gardena pass, I began to feel an itch on my right foot, which was resting on a small lump. I looked down and to my horror saw that my foot was in fact on an ant's nest and the itch was the first few dozen ants exploring above my sock line. Below that, my sock and shoe was unrecognisable, just a black crawling mass of ants. I hate ants. I must of looked a pretty sad figure as I hopped around, attached to my wing, desperately trying to rid myself of these terrible little creatures. It was a pretty low moment. Little did I know it was about to get worse!

With the sky now completely grey and ominous, I figured I better get out of here, even if it was going to be a glide down. I launched again, skimming over the slope towards the low pass. Of course I had not walked as high as I had intended as I'd stopped and thrown out my gear to catch the thermal. I'd curse that decision as I now landed only 40m from the col, but on the wrong side of it. Another 10m of altitude and I'd have cleared it! Once again, I walked to the col with my wing bunched up. I dumped it and unclipped and went to find a launchable spot. The problem was there was a gentle breeze blowing over from the south. I needed to launch on the north side, facing west. There was a gentle gully, and it was below the col itself. The wind was light and with a chalet sheltering me I figured I could manage the cross wind launch down the shallow gulley. All I needed was to be able to glide out to the valley below.

I laid the wing out up against the chalet and put in a concerted run. The forward launch went well, I was off the ground, but the gulley was so shallow I was soon back on the ground, I ran again, hard. Airborne again, but it wasn't over, the ground came to meet me once more and this time I wasn't going to out run it. I ended up in a heap in a muddy area around a cows drinking trough. So close.

Some say that stupidity is repeating exactly the same thing and expecting a different result. By that definition this was one of the most stupid moments in my life. I walked back up the hill, laid out again and attempted the same launch again. Picking myself out of the mud for a second time I saw the obvious solution that had somehow escaped me the first, and second, time. Walking up the north side of this gully meant I could launch higher, off a grassy spine and even into the light southerly wind. As I laid out yet again the overdeveloping sky now started to spot with rain. No big deal I thought as I forward launched into the valley.

As I headed out over a golf course the rain got harder.
And harder. Within the space of about a minute it was pouring
down. It was the sort of rainstorm that sends people skittering
for cover. It was the sort of rainstorm that drenches you in
seconds. I could do nothing but get wet. Very wet. I pointed at
Corvara and hoped the wing would be ok. With a soaked wing
my glide angle was terrible, but I could see I'd make it over the
edge where the road snaked down the pass in a series of tight
hairpins with the town at the bottom. As I descended the glide
looked increasingly touch and go. Several times I considered
turning and landing inside one of the hairpins, but instead I just
managed to glide over the next bit of road, all the time being
drenched by the rain. I was only really alarmed as I saw a car
and caravan come round a hairpin two below me. I judged our
closing speeds and decided I would cross the next bit of road
before he arrived. A crash with a paraglider surely would not be
something he'd be looking out for!

Thankfully as I came closer to the town at the bottom
the hillside became a little steeper. I could see in the centre of
the town the official landing field with a wind sock in the
centre. It was as though it was toying with me – I could see it
but there was no way I'd make it. Instead I had to contend with
the only open space within range to land in which consisted of
a reasonable patch of grass. The only problem was it was on
the wrong side of the cable car station – the side the cables
come out off! I had to squeeze my landing in to the corner of
this already small field.

Exhausted, I lined up the landing, happy to see my Dad
draw up in our team vehicle next to the spot I was about to
land in. With one final mental effort I put the wing down safely
and tried to pack up quickly in the still pouring rain, as though I
could prevent the wing getting even wetter than it already was!

I dumped the wing and harness in the van and climbed

in out of the rain. I was beaten. At that moment, and for the only time in the race, I wanted to give up. I wanted to just close the van door and drive away. I felt like I'd gone from 'hero' to 'zero' in six short hours. I'd given everything mentally and physically and it had not been enough. Poor decisions had compounded poor decisions and I'd ended up losing many hard won places. The final flight down in the pouring rain had been the ultimate insult the weather had thrown at me.

What happened next was quite remarkable. As my Dad set about making some pasta and refuelling me with food, the rain passed and the sun came back out. Two boys, about 11 or 12 years old, turned up at the van door and asked for my autograph. I've never been asked for my autograph before! Then came a local tandem pilot to say hello, followed by another local pilot and his wife who insisted on having a picture of his wife taken with me. Finally the boys came back with cameras asking for photos. Amongst all this I got some food inside me and realised that I could not possibly stop, there were simply too many people following me. My pride was at stake here!

There was no great tactical choice to be made here, I was at the foot of the Gardena pass, my route out of the Dolomites, so the only thing to do was trudge up the pass that everyone who'd gone over my head had flown over. I called Tom who insisted other people had also had a bad day. Paul like me had got stuck and wasn't that far ahead on the other side of the pass and Jouni Makkonen had ended up in a tree further down the valley with his wing ripped. Somehow my fellow X-Alpers hardships did not reassure me – we were all in this together, but it did encourage me to stop mentally beating myself up so much. Nevertheless I arrived at the top of the pass still feeling despondent. From here the valley descended west but the wind was blowing strongly over the pass. I knew from my preparation that there was a 15min walk up to a launchable spot above the valley.

Walking over the Gardena Pass.
Photo: Jörg Mitter/Red Bull Content Pool

Due to the strong wind I decided any take-off would be marginal and the flight probably turbulent. I felt like I'd escaped disaster so many times already on this day that fate needed no more tempting. Reluctantly I turned and walked down the pass. With hindsight it was probably the wrong choice. I probably could have flown it, but my heart was not in it. Despondency was sucking me in. Walking down a valley, with nearly 2000m of descent in total, much of which should have been flown, did nothing to lighten my mood. I was grumpy, unpleasant and at times almost tearful. The tiredness was probably catching up on me too.

As dinner time approached, something clicked in my head. I needed to sort myself out. Dad had gone ahead to cook dinner and I quickly called him to check he'd stopped somewhere with open ground next to it. I was carrying a soaking wet glider with a broken line. The first step to sort my head out was to sort out my gear. I'd open out the wing, fix the line and dry it while I ate the food that was being prepared. Even this didn't quite work as planned. Half way through splicing the new line it started to rain once again. Instead of being able to let my father leisurely pack up the wing while I ate the food, it instead became a mad rush to get the wet glider back in the bag before it got even wetter. Still, getting the wing back in shape had helped, I felt I was ready to face whatever the race would throw at me once again. I was still hanging in there.

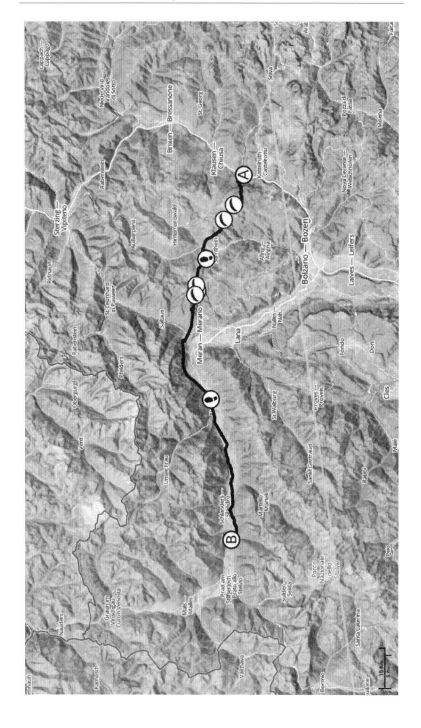

Day 6: Waidbruck to Lasa

The night was spent at Waidbruck in the bottom of the valley that heads north of Bolzano. West of me was the Ritnerhorn, my planned start point for flying. I didn't start early on this day, instead electing for a 5am alarm. By this time there was light in the sky and I was surprised to hear a van draw up next to our camper van (which was in the middle of the village). Sliding open the door revealed a bakery van delivering to the doorstep of the shop opposite. I don't know if he was a race follower or simply a generous person but he gave us a couple of fresh bread rolls. An auspicious start to the day.

It was a tough ascent to the top of the Ritnerhorn. In fact I was initially aiming at the official take off at the top of the cable car station. I'd arranged to meet my Dad there who would come up with my flying clothes and the ever necessary food and water. As I came up the last part of the slope there was a steady thermic breeze blowing up the east face and puffs of cumulus just above the top. It seemed the day was already working. As I came higher I changed my mind, the conditions were weak and the day was early – I favoured launching from the top of the Ritnerhorn itself rather than the cable car station. My uncomplaining father took the fact he'd now have an unexpected hike across a mountain and up a pretty steep slope to meet me without a murmur of dissent.

The main footpath up to the summit was a veritable motorway – obviously trampled by thousands of tourists walking the path from the cable car to the summit of this mountain. It was still early and more or less deserted though as I romped my way along, buoyed with the enthusiasm that reaches all of us as we approach a summit. As I pushed up the last section, short but steep, I was unsurprised to be see two men with a television camera preparing their equipment. By now I was used to meeting the race photographers and film crews in the most unlikely places. I greeted them merrily as I arrived at the top but as I started talking about the race it very quickly became clear they hadn't the faintest idea what I was talking about. It turned out they were nothing to do with the race, they were just there shooting a local documentary!

I laid out the wing to dry and rested a while to watch conditions develop. Gone was the impatience of the previous morning. There was a problem though. Sure, the east face was working, but there was a steady 15 km/h breeze from the west. The cumulus clouds that were forming off of the east face were only tens of meters above the summit and were being blown eastwards pretty swiftly before dissipating. I waited but it wasn't really going to improve, I could launch to the west side but I'd be unlikely to climb here, plus the fact the ground in front was very shallow. After more dithering I launched, circled once in an unconvincing zero before setting off on a glide to the North West. In front of me was a big lump of mountain with its south face towards me. I needed to get onto the west face and figured that if I couldn't climb here then I'd be better off landing and walking over than trying to glide round. As I arrived at the south face the wind did indeed seem to be coming from the west, across the slope. Closer still and there was a little bit of lift, accompanied by singing birds. It wasn't strong enough to work so I continued with the plan of landing on the slope. I approached just above the tree line. The slope in front of me was not particularly steep but littered with boulders.

I was expecting an easy slope landing, the cross wind allowing me to approach in to wind and touch down gently. A short distance away from the slope my ground speed seemed much higher than I expected. Suddenly everything happened fast – the ground was approaching rapidly and I was committed, there were no other options. Still some meters away from impact, my vision became locked on a moderately sized boulder – which was the point at which I was going to connect with the ground. I was going fast now, I was clearly landing downwind! For some reason I put my feet out as I flared as hard as I could. I hit the side of the boulder feet first and bounced over it, before coming to a stop in a heap. Why I put both feet out I don't know, it was an instinctive action, and it seemed the safest thing at the time, but in hindsight could have earned me a broken leg! This time though, I got away with it.

As I stood up it was clear the wind was blowing up the slope and now slightly cross from the other way. The upslope breeze was actually quite reasonable. The light lift with the singing birds had obviously been more than just a blip, it had clearly matured into a quite workable thermal. Still, one wrong turn would have put me below the tree line and a long glide out and round into the valley, so I did not regret the choice of landing. However, as I stood and gauged the conditions the wind once again blew across the slope from the west, the direction I'd expected. Although it was still early there were weak thermals bringing the wind onto the slope. I bundled up the wing and walked up a little way to a point I thought would be better to launch from and waited for the next cycle. The shallow boulder strewn hillside offered no good launch options but I found an area where the risk of catching lines seemed lowest by avoiding the biggest bits of rock. With the wind back up the slope, I forward launched again, or tried to. The rocks made it nearly impossible as the line snagged on the jagged surfaces.

Second time lucky, and I was off again and climbing gently in front of take-off. I'd timed it right, just into a cycle and, although it took a while, I managed to climb up to the height I needed to cross this lump of mountain and get out into the main valley. I worked my way northwards along the west faces, patiently exploring every little bit of lift. Finally, I was close enough to attempt a valley crossing on to the South East faces opposite - my passport to crossing the next line of mountains. This in turn would take me into what I hoped would be an easy run along the Merano valley which runs almost due west for fifty kilometres.

I arrived very low, only a few hundred meters off the valley floor and down around 1400m above sea level. Still it was working and, to the amusement of a group of walkers stopping for a break, I patiently worked weak climbs, gaining a little then losing it again, climbing above their vantage point and then dropping below it again. Finally, I found a more consolidated climb and it took me up higher and I left my new friends behind. Nothing was going to be easy today though and as I climbed to within a few hundred meters of the ridge the climb was blown to bits by the strong west wind blowing over and through a col. I was still a few kilometres from the col and the main ridge but every good consistent climb was blowing me back east away from the direction I needed to go. It was rough too – every time I pushed back west I'd get thrown around violently in this turbulent lee side. After some time playing this game I decided that I'd had enough and I'd land in the highest clearing I could find in the trees and walk the few kilometres over the mountain. With a big clearing on the south face and the trees bending over in the strong west wind the landing was easy enough despite the turbulence.

Still in my harness with my glider next to me I stood contemplating the situation. As I did so the strong wind across the slope became a perfect upwind breeze. Despite the fact this was getting a bit silly, I'm never one to look a gift horse in the mouth, so I quickly pulled the glider up and stepped off the mountain again in exactly the same place I'd landed. I seemed to be making a habit of this today! But it was to no avail. After a rough, wind-blown climb I spent the next twenty minutes getting thrashed around in this most turbulent of places before finally landing back at exactly the same place. If you don't try, you don't find out, but now it was sure I had to walk over this lump so I headed up through the trees to find a path that was marked on my map as taking me over this line of mountains.

Finding the path initially was not so straight forward as I didn't have a great map and the path I was on did not exist. At least not on the map. The main footpaths and walking trails were well marked on the ground so I would know when I reached the path I was aiming for. Soon my path petered out and I cut up through the woodland. I didn't need to go far before seeing a solid fence and a decent forestry track. I thought I'd struck the path I needed but it turned out not to be. This path contoured along the mountain and from checking the altitude on my watch I could see that this could not be the one I was aiming for. It was clearly well used but obviously did not warrant a mention by Italian map makers. I love Italians but they are really not very good at making maps. Frustratingly I had to turn east along this track, even though I needed to go west, because that was the only way I could be sure to intersect the path I needed that would take me up and across the mountain.

Finally I found it and once up and on open ground (now back up around 2000 metres in altitude) I decided to take a direct line figuring it would be quicker. The ground was full of lumps and steeply sloping in places and I soon realised that I'd have been quicker staying on the main path, but the difference was minor and what looked like the col was now in sight.

Even though I had a rubbish Italian map with me I was feeling fairly confident about the area. In front of me I could see a mountain I'd walked up in training. I hadn't managed to fly that day, so I had not seen the area from the air, but I knew that below it to the west was the top station of the Merano cable car (with an official paragliding take off) and below that the ground dropped dramatically to the valley, far, far below (only a few hundred meters above sea level). Logically the high ground to my left as I came through the col was the next spur south from the one the cable car was on, therefore as soon as I reached the other side I would be able to launch. Climbing a fence, I came to a launchable spot with a gentle slope, but there was a family having a picnic, blocking the launch. I didn't really want to ask them to move and in any case if I continued up a little more I'd give myself a bit more height and possibly would be able to see further round to the left. Summitting the next rise and crossing another fence found me in a shallow area with nothing but bracken - horrible stuff to launch on. A barbed wire fence in front gave way to an area of shrubs as the slope became steeper. I considered back tracking and launching next to the family but I'd spent far longer than I had planned walking over here. I needed to get airborne again otherwise I'd miss the best part of the day for flying. Clouds were building strongly and I expected the day to overdevelop so I'd soon run out of time to be able to fly.

I laid the wing out carefully on the bracken and tried to lay the lines so they wouldn't catch. It would be another tricky launch, but there was no danger, the slope was shallow and once I had the wing above me it would be a simple case of running into the air, ideally before the barbed wire fence below me! I still couldn't see round the lump of hill I was on to my left, but I did not give it too much thought as I focussed on pulling the wing into the air for the fourth time that day. The launch went smoothly, and I was soon floating out from the hill bearing left out towards what I thought would be the main valley.

I was wrong. I'd just launched myself into a whole world of trouble. In fact I was now in a narrow steep-sided V-shaped valley filled with pine trees. The valley dropped gently to my left. Too gently; it seemed to go on for kilometres. Far from dropping away steeply to the main Merano valley, instead it seemed to be a hanging valley high up in the mountains and the main valley was actually the other side of the ridge that I was facing across this unlandable space. I sailed merrily past the only clearing easy to land in as I weighed all this up. Fate seemed to be playing with me – I was flying along quite serenely, but at the same time the inevitability of my situation was eating away at me. On the other side, near the cable car station, were open fields. To get into them I'd need more height than I had in order to clear the tree line opposite me. I had to try; it seemed to be my only chance. In theory that side was in the lee but I was hoping it may still offer a little bit of lift to get me over those tree tops and into the field. All I needed was a little bit of luck, and few more meters. As I set off across the glide was quite good, the air was buoyant and I wasn't losing much height – halfway there I began to believe I might actually make it, I almost convinced myself – I was now level with the tree tops and only a few hundred meters away. Then my glide returned to normal, and I sank below the trees – the fields tantalisingly close, but impossible to reach.

Back to reality. I had to land this glider somewhere in the sea of trees below me and there were two criteria. The first priority was that I had to get myself onto the ground safely and the second was that I had to try not to do it in such a way that I'd end up with the glider in trees or badly damaged. I also decided this side of the valley would be best as I'd be able to walk only a very short distance over the ridge to the place I should have walked round to in the first place if I had not been quite so dumb! I spotted it – an area with shrubs allowing me an approach clear of big trees. The terrain was horrible – on a very steep slope and without any clear space at all – but I could see a way to steer the glider in at least so that I could get my feet more or less onto the ground before the glider became entangled. The approach though would be difficult, the narrow gorge did not allow much space to manoeuvre. I lined up as well as I could but I still left myself with an unfeasibly tight last turn to slot the glider into the space. As I threw my weight over and hauled on the brake line to pull the wing round, I knew I'd overdone it. The glider immediately started to spin, instinctively I countered by pulling on the opposite brake, but that only caused the glider to temporarily go into a parachutal stall – stopping all forward movement. This all happened so quickly, and frankly by rights I should have been in the trees. I was lucky though, I was facing away from the slope and the sides of the gorge were very steep. This gave me the vital split second I needed to throw both my hands up and let the wing surge forwards and fly again out into the valley. Disaster averted, but I looked forlornly behind me at the opportunity that had escaped me – I was now too low to try to put the glider in there and I was resigned to flying down the gorge once again.

Back to the game of looking for somewhere to land. On the opposite slope (a long way from the track and where I needed to be, but I was now into survival mode – beggars can't be choosers!) I spied a place where a tree had been chopped down. A single tree. The grassy clearing that was left was incredibly steep, but that was in my favour. The thing that made it possible though was that amongst these tall pines, the trees directly below this gap were mere babies – only a few meters high – combined with the steepness of the slope meant that I had a possible landing approach. It had to be extremely accurate, the space was tiny but the approach was easier than the one I'd just attempted acrobatics to get into. I was still expecting the wing to get tangled in the trees (there simply wasn't the width above me) but I was pretty sure I'd get my feet onto solid ground before that happened. Sure enough I touched down on the grass next to the stump. I immediately looked up as the wing collapsed above me and came tumbling down in a heap to land next to me. Save for a few wing tip lines that were easily pulled out of the small tree beside me, even the wing had not become ensnared by the branches. The relief of being safely back on the ground was counterbalanced by the terrible situation I'd put myself in. The slope was so steep I could barely stand, let alone pack my gear. I was only able to stop things from tumbling down the slope by forcefully jamming them against the uphill side of the tree stump.

Outside of the few meters of clearing I was completely surrounded by dense forest – the sort of forest where the thick tree branches continue all the way down to the ground. Finally, I'd need to climb down this gorge, cross the river at the bottom and then climb back out on the other side. It seemed an enormous challenge but there was no other choice, so I just got on with it. I made it to the river using branches to lower myself down the steepest sections. Luckily the fast flowing river was full of boulders so I could cross it by jumping from one to the next. The opposite bank was so overgrown with bushes that it was impassable, so I had to travel a little way along the river bed until I found somewhere to try to climb the other side. The place I found was clear because of a landslip, not the most auspicious sign, but again, there was no choice. It was so steep I was literally climbing, hauling myself up with my hands and clambering over the skeletons of fallen trees. When there were no dead trees I had to resort to clutching at the earth and the little vegetation there was. As I reached the top of the area that had slipped away I was presented with an overhang to pull myself over – somehow I managed, all the time not daring to look back down at what I'd scrambled up. After that it became easier and after a few hundred slow and painful metres fighting through the undergrowth I emerged on to the well-worn walking track. I felt like a great explorer returning from the wilderness to civilisation after conquering a new frontier. Who was I kidding? In fact I'd just spent the last hour scrambling across a gorge because of my own bad judgement.

Having wasted even more of the flyable day, I now needed to get across to the take off by the cable car station. Arriving there I found a large digger remodelling the slopes around the station, obviously to improve the area for the ski season. The area he was now working looked like it should have been the launch point, at least before it was turned into a mess of mud being hauled around by a big yellow monster. I was beginning to think that maybe today was not really my day. I went to see if there was anywhere on the other side of the cable car building but there was not enough space.

Returning to the slope dominated by the digger, I saw he'd moved a little to the side. I walked down a little way to a point to get out the harness but he waved to me to get out of the area – I showed him the glider bag and made paraglider motions with my hands – he understood and reluctantly let me carry on. I quickly unpacked the glider, the weather really was not on my side now as this was turning into a race against time to get some flying in. There was already overdevelopment to the north of Merano with a mass of cloud bringing light rain and shade across a big area. It was not menacing yet, but big enough to make traversing it on a cross country flight almost impossible. I figured it was unlikely to get better, so I might as well get back in the air and salvage what I could from the day. As I laid out in the mud, a crowd gathered above me to watch me launch. I've never been too fond of crowds, and after all the challenges of the day I just wanted to launch quietly on my own somewhere, but I had no choice, so I simply clipped in and ran off the hill, leaving the crowd behind me and rejoining the solitary world of the cross country paraglider pilot.

I climbed in weak lift heading out to the valley but everything was in shade in this area now. I needed to keep moving despite not even being above take off. I crossed Merano itself, and headed for the south faces. Despite the overdevelopment and shade, the lower slopes were now back in the sun and the valley wind should be blowing up the hill here. Still I was nervous – I'd be arriving low and this big wide open valley was famous for its fruit. Land cultivated for fruit is covered in small trees strung along wires and supported by metal poles. Despite the wide valley this is a terrible area to have to land a paraglider. As I crossed the valley I looked for a place to land, if I needed to. In paragliding it is a psychological error to become focussed on where it is possible to land – if you think about landing you normally do. If you focus on going up you normally go up. Still, sometimes you can't risk it and my technique in these cases is to find a spot that I can land in, log it in my brain, including the height I'd need to leave to get there, and then ignore it and focus on where I need to go to get back up. This time I spotted a building site which looked about the size of a football pitch and open – it was a few kilometres away but in the right direction. With this knowledge, I continued across aiming for a small castle on a knoll below the south facing slopes now towering above me. To my pleasant surprise, I was right for once, and flew straight into a weak but consistent climb. I spent an absolute age drifting in the weakest of lift, gaining only a few hundred meters, but staying in the air was the name of the game. The thermal became so weak I could only just maintain and after spending about 10mins circling at the same altitude I finally began to lose a little height and move on. Maybe half a kilometre further I repeated the experience. Circling in this weak lift I was now close to the south facing slopes that were unfortunately still in shade. With patience I worked my way slowly along this first part of the valley, never getting higher than about 1500m (lower than my take off height) but still airborne, still in the game. As well as the unlandable orchards and the lack of any decent lift, the Merano valley had another danger to test the functioning of my sleep deprived brain: all the way along the valley were cables strung from the valley floor to the buildings clinging to the steep-sided slopes of the mountains. Some were cable cars carrying tourists, others service cable cars, many abandoned and others still simply power cables. In every case they were extremely difficult to see in the grey light. As well as concentrating on the climbs I needed to focus on looking for buildings that looked like they may have cables coming from them and trying mentally to match them up to the equivalent building or pylon below in the valley. Finally, as I lost another weak climb I realised I had to fly out and round a cable and in doing so I left the buoyant air that seemed to be supporting these weak climbs on the corner of the valley. I soon dropped into the valley flow – the wind was blowing up the valley and carrying me where I needed to go, but any chance of climbing away was gone now, the only game to play was chicken with the ground as I tried to eek out the glide downwind.

I'd left the building site I'd identified as a landing option far behind by now, but as I'd flown past it I had seen that it was actually a deep excavation, so it wouldn't have been such a good call after all! Now in front I could see a lorry depot with a forecourt where I'd be able to land but as I dropped lower the wind increased and my glide angle got better. I spotted a small green patch amongst the almost uninterrupted fruit trees ahead of me and decided to continue to this spot. My glide was so good now that I was looking at the ground at such a shallow angle that it was getting difficult to see any open spaces. What is more my ground speed was really very fast. I still had some height as I arrived at the patch I'd identified. Should I continue or not? There might be somewhere a couple of fields further, but it was difficult to see – I continued a little downwind of this patch and passed the point of no return before I could reassure myself that there was indeed a narrow gap between the apple trees up ahead. One turn into wind and I lined up with this gap – running cross wind the gap was no more than twenty metres wide, but with the strong headwind I could almost put the wing down vertically. Even the metal poles that still dotted the open space were easy enough to avoid. So that was it. I was in the village of Naturns, only a third of the way along the valley towards the Stelvio pass. I was jealous of Micheal Gebert and Thomas De Dorlodot who'd flown this valley that I'd now need to walk the length of.

For once the weather was hot and I littered my gear around me, taking what I figured was a well-earned rest. My Dad was stuck in a traffic jam in the village before (I was able to inform him that it was due to an accident on the cross roads in the centre and that the police were letting a few cars go in each direction at a time – I had after all just flown straight over it!). I took off my shoes and let my feet air a little as a car drew up. It was a local pilot who had been tracking me on the live tracking and had come out to greet me. He shared some local knowledge about flying up near the Stelvio pass but neither of us were too optimistic for the next day's weather.

Back to walking, I did consider walking back up the south facing hillsides, but the time was against me and I'd probably only manage a glide down. Even with the valley wind assisting me it was not that likely that it would be much more efficient than just walking particularly when I took into account the rising ground and the fact the wind would drop as evening approached. So walking in the heat of the afternoon it was. Once again there was a cycle path which thankfully kept me off the main road and the afternoon was punctuated by stops for food, water, and on one occasion an impromptu refreshing cold shower rigged up by Dad on the tailgate of the van.

Plotting our route up the Merano valley.
Photo: Olivier Laugero/Red Bull Content Pool

As early evening arrived I chose a narrow track through the apple orchards as the quickest way. My map showed this joined up with the path I needed on the far side, but whether I got the wrong path or, once again, the map was flawed, I don't know. What I do know is that soon the path petered out and I was walking through the orchard with trees either side. Fortunately the trees were planted in more or less straight lines and I was heading in the right direction so I just kept picking my way through until I did finally pop out at the next village. Anybody trying to follow my trace on the live tracking would have had some fun here! Anyhow, with all these shortcuts meeting up with my Dad became about an hourly occurrence as my path intersected with a road or a village. As the day wore on I became more or less obsessed with getting as close to the end of the valley as possible. Simple arithmetic told me that I couldn't reach the foot of the Stelvio pass tonight but I was determined to get as close as I could. As the light began to fade storm clouds were looming once again and when the darkness did finally fall I was once more walking in the rain. Refusing to stop for long I continued pushing as hard as I could. It was probably a little too hard, but I was determined. With a couple of hours to go I started to feel some pain in the side of my foot. The sensible thing to do would have been to stop and change my trainers but I'd set myself some tough targets and I knew where I wanted to get to – I simply had to keep moving to get there.

In fact the pain was on the site of an old blister from training, if I had stopped to think about it, which I didn't, it would have been obvious that I was developing my first blister of the race, almost a week in. Walking this far and this hard day in day out brought with it a certain general level of background pain, which, after a while became quite normal. I suppose my body had just shut it out. I think it is for this reason that I ignored the pain on the side of my foot. It was just a bit more pain – it wasn't important.

The last section was, as always, in the dark, but it didn't stop me taking footpaths still. My goal for the night was a town called Lasa, and it was there that Dad was instructed to go and find somewhere to park the van for the night. Arriving at Lasa I came through an area that was industrial, a large lorry park and big buildings (perhaps a saw mill?) gave way to piles of wood stacked around the track that had now turned into a road. Later, the piles of wood gave way to huge piles of quarried stone.

It was a very spread out village. It is difficult to describe how horrible, how defeating, it is to believe that you've arrived at your goal for the night, only to realise that you haven't yet arrived. Before I got to the outskirts of the village, no matter how weary I was I still had a purposeful stride to my step. Now, however, I kept on expecting to see the van around the next corner, but around each corner was simply another street and another pile of quarried stone. Communication with my Dad seemed to be difficult, just because we were both tired and neither of us really knew exactly where we were in this village, never mind where the other was! Dad had finally parked up at the small railway station and, hearing the despair in my voice as I tried to establish were the station was, he came back to find me. (Our conversation had gone something like, "where are you parked?", "at the station, where are you?", "in the centre of the village by a level crossing – where do I go?", "well, follow the railway", "which way, right or left?", "that depends - which side of the tracks are you on?", "south, I think, which side should I be" and so on until we were both confused). Finally we met up with a few hundred meters remaining to the station car park and the minutes ticking away to the cut off at 11pm. As we walked the last section together I commented that Lasa was not at all what I expected. "Yes" replied Dad, "I know what you mean – it is quite industrial isn't it, not the pretty alpine village I was expecting". "No, no" I replied shaking my head, "that's not what I mean at all, I was expecting somewhere much more dusty, windswept, prayer flags fluttering about, that kind of thing". We were both too tired to laugh at the joke, but I needed the minor escape from reality for just a minute.

Once in the van we inspected my foot. The blister was deep and probably needed draining but we decided that could wait for the morning. I drank my evening bottle of recovery formula, took two Ibuprofen (on top of the paracetamol I'd already taken a little earlier), rubbed my legs in the magic cream we'd picked up on the third day, washed and treated my feet with special foot cream and retired to bed in my compression socks. All this helped my body to recover overnight, and by this point in the race it had become an essential routine just to keep going. Tomorrow my body would need every bit of assistance. Tomorrow I had to tackle the mighty Stelvio pass.

Day 7: Lasa to somewhere on the south side of the Bernina Pass

Arrrgghhhh! Bloody hell that hurts! I was sitting on the bunk in the jack up roof of the camper van with my feet dangling down into the living area below. My Dad was 'operating' on my blistered foot with a scalpel in an attempt to drain it. It was already 4.30am and I wanted to get going but this needed some attention. The problem was that the blister was so deep that draining it was not the simple job of just pricking it with a pin. It required multiple lacerations which didn't seem to be really doing the job. What is more I was not feeling at all well. My stomach swam and I felt distinctly sick, I got Dad to pass up a bowl so if I threw up it would be into that, but as soon as I sat back with the bowl I realised I was not going to throw up. My head was spinning and my vision was beginning to close in. It was worse. I was about to faint if I did not do something quickly. Luckily I was able to gingerly lie back on the bed, still with my feet dangling down, but at least now in a lying position until the moment had passed. I'd be ok, but it was hardly an auspicious start, I'd nearly thrown up, passed out and had my foot cut open and it was still before 5am!

I was not looking forward to today. Thomas and Michael had landed high up on the Stelvio pass at the end of yesterday. I, however, was still in the valley and so I'd have to walk up it this morning. It was over 2000m of ascent and first I needed to get to the bottom of it, which in itself was several hours walk. Furthermore, Clement Latour (FRA 3), my friend and competitor, was not far behind me.

Once the foot incident was out of the way I pushed on hard. Despite it still being early a couple of local pilots drove up to say hello and Olivier Laugero, one of the race photographers, seemed to have been assigned to me on this day as he kept appearing at random moments and shooting off hundreds of photos. It was on this early morning part of the walk that I found myself walking down a die straight road with telegraph wires looping from pole to pole along one side. It reminded me of the opening sequence to a TV programme that my brother and I used to watch when we were young, 'The Littlest Hobo'. Feeling somewhat inspired I pulled out my phone and posted the rather appropriate lyrics of the theme tune as a diary entry, complete with a photo of the view down the road that had sparked it all: Down this road/ That's where I wanna be/ Every stop I make/ I make a new friend/ can't stay for long/ Just turn around and I'm gone again/ maybe tomorrow... I let the lyrics trial off at 'maybe tomorrow'. I was thinking maybe tomorrow I'll fly far, but the inspiration dried up. This early morning moment of spontaneity then triggered all sorts of responses from the guest book over the next few days, including additional versus and multiple 'littlest hobo' references! These fun and games certainly helped while away the kilometres!

I had wolfed down a second breakfast in the village at the bottom of the main road up the pass. Now I was ready to take on the mighty ascent of the Stelvio. Soon after starting to walk once again I passed under the road sign announcing that the pass was open and I resigned myself to the gruelling push this would be. The first part, up to the town of Trafoi, was more or less straight, so I stayed on the main road. At least it was straight on the map. Coming out of a half tunnel (it was open on one side – there to protect the road from avalanches) I found the road did two short and sharp hairpins. I looked back at the map. The tunnel was marked, but no hairpins. How a 1:50,000 scale map can simply ignore a major feature like this escapes me. Don't get me started on Italian maps again! I passed our van parked at the side of the road with Dad asleep in the driver's seat. Bless him, he was tired and I didn't actually need anything from him so I just kept on walking leaving him to his snooze. I would get told off for this later, when he woke and couldn't see me on the road up to where he was, but never mind.

On a long ascent like this we found that one of the most important things was simply keeping my spirits up. I was now approaching the village that my Dad had decided was called 'Ohmygod'. (Which seemed appropriate, although how he got that from its real name of 'Gomagoi' is beyond me – it isn't even an anagram for goodness sake!) We were still being shadowed by race photographer Olivier Laugero and he'd recommended to my Dad to get some of the local ham and cheese from the bakery in 'Ohmygod'. It was still quite early in the morning, but having already consumed pretty much all our breakfast options in different sittings through the morning, my Dad thought that this would make an interesting alternative 'between meals' snack compared to the normal energy bars. And so it was that he walked down towards me as I approached the town with a platter of local produce held on his fingertips at shoulder height, waiter style, enquiring whether, "would sir care to try any of the local delicacies?" Indeed I did. It was, without doubt some of the best ham and cheese I have ever tasted.

On reaching Trafoi I left the road to ascend the mountain via a footpath that took a more direct route up. However this path would eventually join the ridge a kilometre or so to the north and higher than the col that the road passed through. I was armed with a plastic bag full of the local ham and cheese and some of the local spiced bread. Despite the worst of the ascent still being in front of me I was ready for this now. I decided to take the path for two reasons. Firstly the road consists of hairpin after hairpin (about 40 of them in fact), and for the first part these were in the forest, so offering little opportunity to short cut them. Secondly, I had a premonition. I'd been to the top of this pass in training. On that occasion the weather had been poor and the wind on the other side was blowing from the north, through the Umbrail pass. I had walked up a slope and launched but I'd been unable to fly out of the pass because the first section of the valley on the other side is actually rather flat before finally dropping. By taking this direct path I'd have an additional 200m to ascend but I was more or less assured a clear glide out if it was flyable.

All good thinking but that was still a few hours away. The path up was actually rather pleasant but the weather was more akin to spring than summer. I was on the lee side of the ridge and the weather would turn from sun to being engulfed in cloud in a few moments. Some of the showers were hard and they came on quickly so I seemed to be endlessly pulling on my waterproof and then taking it off again. As I climbed higher the sunny intervals seemed to get a bit longer and on more than one occasion I stopped in a clearing on this sunny slope with a lovely upslope breeze in my face and contemplated the improbable: flying it. It was, on balance, utter madness, but then this whole race was madness. Clearly the air mass was very unstable and the sunshine was bringing thermic air up the slope. I also knew I was in the lee, but I figured I'd be able to launch, climb in the upslope breeze and land again on this slope, well below the turbulence of the top ridge that would be caused by the wind coming over the other side (I still had over a 1000m of mountain above me). The mountainside above was fairly open so landing again would not be an issue, but below was forested back down to Trafoi, which I had passed about an hour before and now resembled nothing more than a model far, far below me. Each time I stopped to consider it, I waited and felt the sunshine on my face, and then, after a few more minutes watched the rain clouds gathering on the mountain to the north before becoming engulfed again. I figured that there were periods of about 10mins of sunshine which were then followed by sometimes extended periods of rain. I weighed up the pros and cons. If I could thermal up I'd save maybe an hour walk, but the gain of time would not be considerable when you add in getting prepared, waiting for the moment and then packing up again. On the downside there was an equally high chance I was wrong and the upslope breeze was too weak, in which case I'd end up back at Trafoi far below and probably kicking my gear around in a terrible tantrum. It simply wasn't worth it. I had to keep trudging up the mountain.

About half way up this stretch was a small mountain hut with a track access. It had modern windows which were steamed up. From that, and the laughter and jovial voices, it sounded like there was quite some group inside enjoying themselves snuggled inside their warm and cosy mountain hut. Although I was only meters away from them as I walked past the hut their world seemed a million miles away from mine. I pushed on past the hut, spotting a fresh iceberg lettuce bobbing about in a water trough. I did a double take. This bright green crispy lettuce seemed rather out of place on this grey cloud covered rocky mountainside. I wasn't in the mood for any lettuce so I just left it to continuing its incongruous bobbing. It must have been left behind after some hysterical salad preparation!

Onwards and upwards, and finally a familiar figure came into view. It was my friendly photographer, Olivier. By now we were very high, close to 3000m and it was extremely cold. Once again I was walking in my down jacket, but I didn't have a hat. So far today every time I'd met Olivier on the road he had insisted I put on a woolly hat with the race logo on (anything for the sponsors), something he carried with him for exactly that purpose. For the first time, here at the top of the mountain I was glad of it. As we made our way along the ridge path that tracked back towards the col where the road passed through, Olivier kept raving about how 15mins before there were beautiful views of the glacier behind and that it would have made stunning photos. 'Would have', because now we could only see a few meters in front of us due being once again engulfed in thick cloud.

Engulfed in cloud.
Photo: Olivier Laugero/Red Bull Content Pool

By now I was cold, exhausted and over-hungry. All I could think of was continuing down to the col for some hot food. I was regretting my choice of path as now I'd just need to descend so the extra height gain was for nothing. My Dad was at the col and if the truth be told I was a bit grumpy that he was not here, but I hadn't asked him to be and most of the time he seemed to be pretty much telepathic about being where I needed him so it was rather unreasonable of me to be grumpy. Still, that logic was lost on me at the time!

I think a photographer's role is to only to observe and record, but Olivier helped me here. He convinced me to take a look on the other side of the ridge where he'd seen a perfect launch spot on his way up. The cloud seemed to have thinned out a bit now and suddenly it did indeed seem that launching would be possible. I could see the valley bottom – it was clear below me so I threw out my wing and prepared my harness. It only takes me a couple of minutes to be ready but in that time the cloud swept in again and started chucking wet snow at me. I threw the harness on top of the still folded wing in a desperate attempt to try to keep the wing dry. The main problem, though, was me. Despite full flying gear, including down jacket, waterproof and speed arms, I was absolutely freezing. So I curled up on top of the harness. Two other photographers had joined Olivier and they seemed to find my bedraggled and exhausted state quite a photo opportunity. I didn't care. At that point I could not think ahead at all, I couldn't see past the snow and the cold.

Waiting to fly.
Photo: Olivier Laugero/Red Bull Content Pool

Then, as if by some divine intervention, the clouds lightened and then cleared. It was still snowing but I could see the ground below me again. I was cautious, flying in snow is not too smart but Olivier was egging me on and in any case it was getting lighter. I did not want to miss this window of opportunity.

Take off on the Stelvio.
Photo: Olivier Laugero/Red Bull Content Pool

The launch was deceptively difficult. The flat area was actually covered in small razor-sharp rocks that clung onto the lines and risked ripping my lightweight wing. I laid out and hauled the wing up in a reverse launch, but one side caught and before I knew it the wing was in a heap at my side. On grass this would have been no issue, but here was a different matter. I had to get out the harness and carefully lay out again. This time I opted to forward launch. The lines caught again, but this time they were the centre lines and with a hefty tug they came free with the wing still more or less in the right shape so I pushed hard on the risers and powered off of the mountain. Airborne at last, what a feeling of exhilaration! I felt like I did on my first soaring flight some 20 years earlier. I whooped with joy and waved goodbye to my photographer friends. Five minutes before I'd been a pathetic figure, crippled by exhaustion, now I was a superhero again, gliding effortlessly over the highest pass in Europe.

Flying out towards Bormio.
Photo: Olivier Laugero/Red Bull Content Pool

The exhilaration soon turned to concentration and then to trepidation. My gamble was paying off, because the extra height was going to allow me to clear the high plateau and fly out into the gorge that led down the Italian side towards Bormio. However, there was not going to be many meters going spare as I approached what was the aerial equivalent of flying over a raging waterfall. The trepidation was due to the 20kmph tail-wind. This meant the wind was spilling down through the gorge exactly like water would be pummelling down a mountain stream. As I came over the edge the road zig-zagged wildly below me, descending a near vertical slope, meanwhile high voltage power lines that had been on my left now seemed to decide that half way up the cliff on the right side of the valley was the best place to be. Someone was having a laugh here, as if flying down a horrible gorge with a strong tail-wind wasn't enough, they had to add power lines into the mix just to make it really interesting. With the waterfall effect the wing felt mushy, I was in strongly sinking air and so it was somewhat delicately that I crossed the power lines close to the pylon at the top of the drop. If it is close I always choose to cross obstacles like this next to a pylon as between the pylons it is nearly impossible to really judge how far you are from the certain death that a collision with high voltage lines would entail. As it was, I had plenty of clearance, but I felt I needed it as there was no telling what could go wrong in this unpredictable air. Having successfully got myself into this gorge, and cleared the lines I was rapidly coming to the conclusion that I didn't want to be here. The road snaked along the left hand side of the gorge, about half way up the hillside. Where it wasn't passing through tiny tunnels bashed through the rock, it was covered by galleries to protect the road from avalanches and rock falls. The right hand side was effectively a cliff with the power lines clinging to it about half way up, and in the bottom the two met in a raging torrent of a river. I had about 5kms to fly to get out of this place and there were no places to land in the bottom. With my current glide ratio I wasn't going to make it out so I had to start working out my options. It didn't take me too long to work out that the only 'get out of jail' solution would be to land on the roof of the avalanche protection on top of the road. I hoped it wouldn't be needed, but knowing that was the only reasonable option allowed me to keep an eye on the road making sure I stayed safely above it as I glided along the valley, fortunately it was descending at about the same rate as my glide ratio.

Just when I was preparing for the worst things started to look up. The strong sink now eased off completely and my glide suddenly felt more normal. I started looking ahead towards the corner to judge if I could make it to Bormio. The power lines rather unhelpfully decided to switch sides of the valley again down here, but now with the extended glide there was a small clearing in the bottom which I could use if needed, so I pushed on and all of a sudden, hallelujah, I was going up! First rule of encountering lift where you don't expect it – circle first, think second! So I started circling and climbed slowly but quite benignly in what was now clearly convergence. There was obviously a light valley flow coming up from Bormio and meeting this cold air washing down the pass. I was saved!

The convergence didn't take me all that high, but it was enough to get out of this dreaded gorge and into the relative sanity of the Bormio valley. I seemed to have struck lucky here because as I came round the corner to turn up the valley that led to the Viola pass, the sun was shining and I hooked into a rather nice 2m/s thermal. Whilst it was indeed true that the sun was shining here, it was not shinning where I needed to go: about five kilometres up the valley a wall of grey indicated a mass of rain. Oh well, I thought, and actually left the thermal, despite that fact it was still going up nicely as I figured any higher would just take me into the horrid weather. As it was the wind was now a tail wind in this valley and, although not too bad at my height, I could see trees thrashing around below me. The glide wasn't too great, but I hit some more weak lift a few kilometres further on and so found myself climbing again, kicking myself for being too impatient and leaving the stronger climb early. It felt like a game of cat and mouse as I charged towards the wall of grey, carried along by the strengthening tail wind as the valley floor rose up to meet me on my glide. Suddenly the ground was coming up very fast indeed as I crossed over the roofs of the village of Semogo. There were no good landing spots so I aimed at a very steeply sloping field facing smack into the valley wind. I was hurtling towards it a considerable speed but if I turned too early I'd simply miss it because it was too steep. At the very last moment I hooked the glider hard left banking it up tightly and connecting with the ground just as the glider came round into wind. It was not elegant, and I deliberately hit the ground quite hard, but I was down and safe just as the sky started spitting with rain. I was feeling a little smug about my judgement as I started to pack up, until I realised a couple of minutes later as I started walking that the spots of rain had been just that – they hadn't come to anything much at all. In fact everything was a bit brighter. I cursed not spending a bit more time in that good thermal and flying further along this valley.

Now, I'd spent more than 4 hours without any support

and despite Dad's best efforts he was still some way behind me. If you've ever driven the Stelvio pass you'll know that the road is not for the faint hearted. Hurtling downwind through the gorge on a paraglider would be considerably quicker at the best of times, but in this case it was made doubly difficult for my Dad to keep up by a traffic jam in one of the less vehicle-friendly holes in the rock that masquerades as a tunnel. I was plodding along the road when he finally caught up with me about 20mins after landing. Overcoming the urge to stop immediately I told Dad to drive on as far as he needed and then to stop and cook the biggest bowl of pasta the world had ever seen. I was the hungriest I have ever been in my life.

Dad and I had spent some time in this area and we had a good idea of where we were going and where the single track road led away from the main road up towards the Viola pass (which has no road over it). The problem was it was also one of the very few bits of the route we didn't have a map for. Between me and the point I needed to leave the road it did two giant hairpins. There was no way I was going to walk around that lot, so as soon as I could see the road doubling back above me I struck off up the steep banking in order to cut the corner. Google Maps on my smart phone at least showed me the form of the road so I could be sure I was heading in the right direction. It was so steep in places I was practically climbing, using my hands and feet, when I popped back out onto the road. The other side of the road had a chalet and a small field with goats and above that a pine forest. I wasn't going to be beaten though and take the road round so I made my way up the edge of the field and negotiated my way over an electric fence onto a small track. I was now running parallel to the road I needed to be on but a bit below it. Cutting through dense fir trees is insanely hard going so I kept on the track looking for a better option. It was about this point the phone rang. 'Err, where are you?' In trying to focus on taking the optimum route by foot I'd overlooked the fact that Dad was waiting on the road with a heap of food ready for me. 'Not on the road' I replied rather sheepishly. It didn't take long to make a new plan to meet up on the road further up, and Dad was now becoming something of an expert in driving the campervan part way through cooking, with the cooking pots wedged in places so they wouldn't slide around. Once we did meet up the food, dry clothes and brief rest was just what was needed to get me back on track.

As I walked away from the van up the road, Sylvan Dhonneur, Clement's supporter, came past me. There was just chance to glimpse a brief wave in the nanosecond that he was in view before he sped off out of sight. He was checking out the route ahead of Clement who was still not too far behind, having had more or less the same flight as I had, despite the fact that he had not been able to out glide the high plateau, having instead to walk up the side of the valley to launch again before finally descending into the turbulent gorge that I'd flown through.

After all the excitement of successfully negotiating the highest pass in the Alps, flying down the other side and living to tell the tale I was back to some rather mundane walking. I'd walked the Viola pass in training and it is quite the opposite to the Stelvio: where the Stelvio was steep sided and rocky, the approach to the Viola was along a shallow grassy valley, sloping gently up to the 2300m col that finally would mark my entry into Switzerland and the third country in my race across the Alps. Technically I'd already passed into Switzerland, as the ridge I'd crossed at the top of the Stelvio separated Italy from Switzerland. Where I'd launched from then was Switzerland, but I'd only really nicked the corner because a matter of meters away I was back into Italy.

I reached the top of the 2300m pass by late afternoon and, once again, with the advantage of an earlier trip, I knew that to fly out from the pass I needed to leave the path and tackle the col at the north side, gaining a bit more height in the process but giving me a fighting chance to launch and glide out of the hanging valley that connected into the main valley system that joined the lower Italian valleys with St Moritz via the Bernina pass. It was still grey and there were clouds clinging tenaciously to the hillside all around. As I crested the col there was no discernible wind but it was starting to spot with rain so I threw the wing out and got ready to launch. Annoyingly a light breeze started to blow down the hill, but it was only very light and I didn't want to give the rain a fighting chance, so I felt that launching was the best policy, despite the fact it required a pretty sustained run to get off the ground.

I seemed to be becoming rather too blasé about launching in rather inappropriate places. As I glided serenely out around a rocky outcrop it occurred to me that a couple of hundred meters more altitude would not have gone amiss. In front of me were trees and no obvious clearing as far as I could see. I was in a bowl with a small lake at the bottom. I figured I could just clear the trees in front of me but the ground did not look like it sloped away very much on the other side of them. I could just see myself gliding on in vain, with no clearings to land in, skimming tree tops and willing my glide to exceed that of the slope until finally the inevitable happened and I crashed ungainly into the trees. Despite the visions of doom, the odds were I'd have managed to out glide the slope, but I wasn't going to try it. I felt like I'd already taken a chance once today with the touch and go glide through the Bormio gorge of death, and I'd got away with it, so I wasn't going to tempt faint a second time. Instead I played nicely, and turned towards the small lake and the clearing there. I executed a 270 degree turn over the lake in order to lose a bit of height and land on the small clearing. The scene was beautiful with the forest and the glassy smooth water just below me as I almost skimmed the surface on the final approach. Still, there was no time for sightseeing, as I hadn't flown much of the valley it was back to walking, albeit downhill for a change. It occurred to me that this was the first time I'd actually walked *down* a hill since the Gardena Pass in the Dolomites.

Later, when I met up with Dad, he asked me why I'd walked round in a perfect circle. I was a little confused until I realised that he was talking about the landing approach over the small lake. My whole flight must have been so close to the ground that the live tracking system hadn't even clocked me as flying, so it had appeared to anyone following that not only had I walked round in an almost perfect circle, about half of it was done walking on water!

It was now early evening. I'd been on the go non-stop since before dawn and exhaustion was beginning to set in. For most of the field coming this way there was a key decision to be made here. The next 'turn point' we had to touch was an imaginary 6km diameter cylinder centred on Piz Palu on the other side of the valley. The first option was to turn south. This way was downhill and the turn point could be touched by simply crossing to the other side of the valley, contouring around. This route would take us to the Sondrio valley to the south, a convenient east-west valley system (the route was more or less due west at this point). Alternatively, it was possible to head north over the Bernina pass (yet another 2300m alpine pass) into the St Moritz valley. If I had to make a decision here then heading south would indeed have been attractive, after such a hard slog the relative ease of the low route via Sondrio was very tempting. Luckily for me there was no choice to be made, no decisions to ponder over. There were plenty of places on the route were there were valid decisions that had to be made depending on weather, time of the day and many other aspects , but for me this wasn't one of them. Back in June I'd checked out both routes. In the comfort of my living room I'd carefully measured the distance I'd need to travel in both cases if I had to walk it all (i.e. worst case) and then looked at the flying options. Bottom line, although it wasn't immediately obvious from looking at the map, was that the route via St Moritz was 20km shorter and provided significantly more flying opportunities (it was surrounded by more or less treeless mountain slopes, launchable from almost anywhere). Even when I took into account the additional effort from the 600m height gain to get over the Bernina pass, it was quicker. In fact the only thing that could have made me take the south route was if I'd been lucky enough to sail through here on my glider in the middle of the afternoon on an epic flying day. As that hadn't happened, the north route it was. Funnily enough the only other person who had taken this route was Thomas De Dorlodot, everyone else had headed south. Although I didn't know it then, this foresight was to prove crucial in the coming days.

I skirted the mountainside to join the main route towards the Bernina pass as high as I could to minimise the misery of having to painstakingly regain height I'd just merrily walked off from descending from the Viola Pass. As I re-joined the road I also reconnected with Dad who had had another rather long drive round, although it did provide the small bonus of passing through a tax free area of Italy where fuel was about half price. Needless to say the van was topped up to the brim. As I scoffed the last of another huge bowl of pasta the darkness started to close in. I'd rather ambitiously set my heart on reaching the top of the Bernina pass and therefore the Piz Palu turn point by close of play at 11pm. I donned a head torch and looked at my map. There were some paths which shortcut the switchbacks, but they were poorly marked and seemed rarely trodden so I chose not to risk getting lost in the darkness of the night and instead took a less conformist approach by cutting the hairpins wherever felt easiest while staying relatively close to the road. This wasn't as easy it sounds. There was no moon out and the night really was pitch black. Even with an excellent head torch it is difficult to see more than a few meters ahead. The road was used infrequently at this time of night and when a car did pass I had to concentrate hard as the headlights swung across the hillside to see a route through the next part, guessing where the road went next and then recalibrating once the headlights came into view above me on the next beat of the road. At one point I set off across a rough field, but the ground became extremely steep. I hoped there would be no wall or other impassable obstacle as I clambered through the blackness of the night. Just when I was beginning to think I'd got it all horribly and hopelessly wrong headlights came into view above me and I could see the road once again.

As the time ticked past my ambition of reaching the pass was slipping from my grasp. Finally we stopped for the night in a small lay-by before the last push to the top. It was bitterly cold at this altitude. The wind had picked up and the van shook as the wind swirled around us. As bad as the weather was it was about to get a whole lot worse!

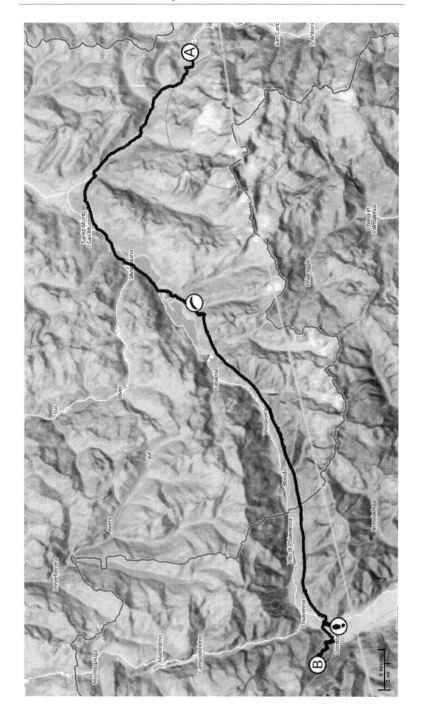

Day 8: Bernina Pass to half way up the Forcola Pass

'Right, got everything?' 'Yep' I said as I turned towards the back of the van to set off for the Bernina Pass. It was first light; after a tough day yesterday I needed a bit of extra rest so I had only started at 5am. Still, that was early enough for most people. As I went to take my first step my Dad lent across and took my shoulders in a firm but fatherly way and turned me gently 180 degrees towards the front of the van, with the remark, in a slightly amused voice, that it was 'this way'. I paused, and with a grin told him, yes indeed, the road to the top of the pass went that way but I wasn't planning on taking the road! Instead my first task of the day was to ascend a heinously steep boulder strewn slope behind the van which connected to the straight part of road directly above us that went to the top part of the pass. With that, I set off in the original direction.

The top of the pass was horrible: a strong north wind was blowing straight into my face and sub-zero temperatures meant I was walking once again in clothing more suited to the ski season than summer in the Alps. At least I was walking along the road here and so every 20mins or so I'd meet up with my Dad who would provide hot coffee, great slabs of chocolate and anything else that could help to alleviate the pain. Just when I thought the weather could not get any worse, it did. Along with the howling wind now came quite heavy wet snow.

Whilst I was trudging along in my winter gear with my head bowed against the elements, hood pulled down against the freezing cold, I noticed that Dad was only wearing a shirt and shorts inside the van. This struck me as odd until I realised he needed to have the heater on full blast inside the van with the blower also on full in order to dry my shoes and clothes from the day before. The irony of him sitting in a sauna whilst a few meters away I was freezing cold seemed rather cruel on both of us!

Sheltering behind the campervan on the Bernina Pass.
Photo: Richard Chambers

Tom, our fantastic weather forecaster and strategist provided an analysis of the weather. Despite strong north east winds the weather was apparently going to be quite good, and the day would have 'some flying opportunities'. The term 'some flying opportunities' bounced around my head during those long hours walking through that blizzard on the top of the Bernina pass. The more I thought about it the more ridiculous it became, until it seemed entirely removed from any kind of reality. I felt downcast, washed out. I needed some kind of revival, a reset.

Entirely by chance I was about to pass right by a campsite I'd stayed in whilst checking out the area. The campsite, Camping Plauns was run by a paraglider pilot and avid X-Alps fan and more importantly had amazing wash facilities to clean up in. A badly needed second shower of the race was on the cards. After a quick wash and change of clothes I was soon sitting behind the counter of their little campsite shop, with a plate of food (some of which had come straight off their shelves) in front of the internet looking at the race live tracking. I was being treated like a king and I was hugely grateful for their kindness, but unfortunately the stay was necessarily short. I had to get back on the road. Now down into the valley the weather was looking up, still windy with clouds scooting across the sky from the north but still there might be, 'some flying opportunities' after all.

Walking through Pontresina a car pulled over to greet me and the driver announced she was Micheal Gerbert's fitness trainer, and she happily handed me a croissant. I didn't really need the croissant having just eaten a whole load of food at the campsite, but I was working on the principle that the more I could eat the more energy I'd have, so I pretty much ate everything anybody handed me without asking questions. It was a strategy that seemed to be working. Eat all the time. Simple and effective. I was vaguely impressed that Michael actually had a fitness trainer. It seemed rather more professional than my approach!

Frustratingly the positive effects of the brief respite in the campsite seemed to be rapidly wearing off. A simple shower and dry clothes couldn't overcome the fatigue of more than a week on the go. It was after 9am in the morning as I cut the corner of the valley heading towards St Moritz itself. There were lots of people out walking in the morning sunshine, enjoying the paths through the forest in the valley floor. Amongst all these people I was mentally struggling. I couldn't work out if I should fly or walk. I could cut up the hill from the corner – it would give me a good launch spot facing into the wind, that is, if the wind wasn't too strong. On the other hand if the wind was too strong up there I'd more or less have to come straight back down again. After passing most of the day walkers with my striding style I now sat despondently on a bench studying a map somehow wanting it to tell me what to do. The walkers I had passed on the path now ambled past me, serving only to highlight my indecision and make me feel even more useless. I was sure I should have gone up the mountain but now I was past the optimum point to do so and I figured going back wasn't worth it. I tried to convince myself it wouldn't be flyable in any case and trudged on.

About this time Thomas had contacted me by phone – he was much further along the valley from me – probably 4 hours ahead of me and had met up with some local pilots who would show him a launch on the south side of the valley above the Maloja pass. He was concerned about the wind. Where I was it was not too strong in the valley, so I passed on the information. It was great to be not too far from someone who approached the race in this way. Sharing information could help us both and more importantly keep us both safe. A little later he called me again, having now reached the launch site. He told me it was extremely windy, but he was going to give it a go anyway. I wished him luck and told him to stay safe. I really was hoping he had a great flight even if it would open up his lead from me. He was too far ahead of me for me to make it to his take off and somehow I didn't seem to be thinking straight today. My decision making abilities seemed to have left me.

Striding into a busy car park next to a church with a rather crooked tower in St Moritz I was impressed to see our van in a parking space right next to where the footpath came out with an empty space on the side with the sliding door. Sometimes it is the little details that make you happy! I dumped my gear against the van, effectively blocking anyone else using that space and flopped into the van for the necessary pit stop.

As I was sat there looking at the map, almost ready to go again, a car pulled up in front of the van. My first, rather grumpy, thought was that they wanted the space but then the passenger door opened and a large figure, previously invisible on account of the fact he was lying almost horizontal with the seat laid back, levered himself out of the car. He was a giant of a man, and although he didn't introduce himself, I recognised him immediately as Alex Hofer, two times X-Alps Champion. Hofer would have been in this race aiming for the hat-trick if it hadn't been for a serious injury in training. He was now in a full body brace and obviously movement was difficult, but apart from that he seemed to be in good spirits. He was there to do some fishing, but had obviously not been able to resist following up on the race just a tiny bit! After exchanging a few words I set off on my way, resigned to walking despite the fact the decision didn't sit easily on my shoulders.

As I walked away from the van I realised I hadn't taken a picture for the on line diary. Even though it was only 20m, retracing my footsteps felt somehow sacrilegious, but it was worth it to get the photo for the diary. Many pilots refer to brilliant and talented pilots like Hofer as 'sky gods' and in a peculiar way he did appear to us like some kind of divine vision. After I left, obviously sensing the unease and uncertainty in our strategy for the day, Alex apparently took the map from my father and looked at the valley and the sky and finally pointed to a low slope above the village of Sils, which faced into the valley wind, and announced nonchalantly that if it was him he'd walk up there and soar the slope in the valley wind before heading downwind. The sky god had spoken.

Meanwhile I was busy walking along the road side. It was a pretty walk but every step seemed to get harder and harder. I passed Hofer and his father once again further along, this time they were stood at the edge of one of the lakes some way away from the road, so we only waved from a distance as I strode onwards and they continued doing what they'd come to do - fish.

Walking along the lake between Silvaplana and Sils was stunning despite it being a rather busy road with no verge or footpath. A TV camera filmed me and a helicopter took some rather impressive footage as I traipsed along the lake. By now my father had passed on to me the revelation from Hofer, so with still some lingering doubt we decided to head for the hill above Sils.

Thomas called. He was alive, which seemed to me to be the most important thing. Furthermore the reason for him calling me, for which I am to this day immensely grateful for, was to pass on information which would help to keep me alive too. He had flown and the thermals were good with plenty of lift heading west along the valley towards Chiavenna. The problem was the wind. At 2500m he had been blown backwards with around 50kmph of wind at that altitude. He'd flown passed Chiavenna (where he said the wind was strongest) and had landed near the top of Lake Como, in the lee of the hills there in the hope that they would provide some shelter from the wind. Indeed they had but, predictably, they had also provided severe turbulence and he'd spent much of the descent over the lake in the pretty firm belief that odds were he'd end up crashing in it anyway and it might just save his life. Fortunately it didn't come to that. He'd just put in an immense flight on a difficult day.

Back in the St Moritz valley, the end of my lake came into sight as I found out for the first time in my life that it is actually just about possible to fall asleep whilst walking. My decision making ability must have been returning because as I met up with Dad once again, I realised I did need to fly out of this valley but I was in no state to do it. There was plenty of the day left and the biggest priority was to get some rest. A 30 min power nap was, for the first time in the race, required. It was at this most inappropriate moment that a TV crew appeared and asked for an interview. A short one I told them, and after answering a few questions on my plans I closed the door and lay back, instantly falling asleep. They continued to film me sleeping through the van's window. Typical, I'd spent 8 days slogging away in the mountains and the first footage they have of me is me having a nap!

Revived from my sleep but rather groggy still, I set off up though the village towards the hill. Dad was going to walk this one with me which was lucky because after a while I realised I didn't have my sunglasses so the poor chap had to run back to the van for them. While he was away I passed Nietszche's house. I found out later that this had been his summer home for a time and some of his works were written here. Nietszche famously wrote that 'all truly great thoughts are conceived by walking' and by this account I figured I should be a genius by the end of this race! Still he also wrote 'that which does not kill us makes us stronger' which was all well and good but I wasn't yet convinced that this race wouldn't kill me.

While I was labouring up this hill the race journalist, Hugh Miller called me for an audio interview. I agreed to give the interview but wasn't prepared to stop walking (I felt I'd wasted too much time already today). The result was rather poor in terms of sound quality due to the heavy breathing on my part! Still after the interview was finished, he told me, 'bloody well done' and that I was doing an incredible job. It was a timely compliment as my morale still needed a bit of a boost.

Above the village the green fields carpeted the undulating ground and I felt like I was in my native English countryside rather than the Alps, but soon the fields gave way to the tree covered slope and we made our way up a path which more or less ascended a spine sticking into the valley. It was quite windy and - more importantly - it was also gusty. I despondently sat down on a bench unsure whether it was even worth going higher. I tucked into a Mars bar whilst Dad bounded up the next 100m or so to see how it was higher up and to see if he could find a clearing to launch from. He was desperate to help and find a solution to fly, and I think he was confident in the plan as it was based on advice imparted to him some hours before by Hofer. He convinced me it wasn't too bad at all and finally I convinced myself that actually the face would be OK as here we were on the spine where the wind would be accelerating around the corner. We were still some 5km upwind of the point Thomas had launched from above the Maloja pass some hours earlier. Dad showed me the clearing he thought was launchable which I quickly dismissed as being too close to the spine. We contoured across the face, off the path now, before we came to another clearing. It was just about perfect. I'd be launching standing on a rock with a boulder field below me, but with the strong wind that wouldn't be an issue. Unsure of what I was doing launching with 50 km/h of wind above me in the big mountains, I pulled the wing up, steadied it, turned and stood momentarily, wing above me, contemplating the world in front of me. Hell, let's do this I thought, and I stepped off the mountain.

No matter how nervous I get on the ground, before launching in a competition, or taking off into marginal conditions, I always immediately relax in the air. I feel at home under the wing, it is almost part of me, and as I glide gracefully upwards all the stress ebbs away from my body. Even today, when I had every reason to be stressed in the air, I was at once relaxed as I soared effortlessly up in the dynamic lift. I could have been soaring a hill side in England, but the difference was that once I reached the top I had to go somewhere else, and there was no telling what that somewhere else would be like! Heading down the valley towards the Maloja pass meant dropping onto the next spine. Without much height from soaring the first ridge I'd come in low, but, whilst this second spine did not have such an obvious face to soar up, it did connect with the mountain behind. I was soon established in a surprisingly normal thermal. The surprising thing was that it wasn't blown apart by the wind and the drift wasn't even that extreme – I was only reading about 15-20km/h of wind on my instruments. Maybe I was worrying about nothing. But then again maybe not – I remained on my guard.

I took that climb to about 2500m, which was not all that high given the valley floor was at 1800m here. Still, it had drifted me towards the pass and now it was time to turn and glide across it. It was a strange pass, because the ground was almost flat on the St Moritz side, but facing towards Chiavenna the ground fell away steeply. I crossed the pass with some trepidation. Instinct plus the crucial information from Thomas told me life was about to get a whole lot more interesting. Indeed it did. Crossing the pass itself was rather benign but after that my ground speed accelerated considerably. Luckily the air I was flying through was also extremely buoyant, so I zoomed along with a strong tail wind and virtually losing no height. The mountain to the south of me was surrounded by cloud just a few hundred meters above my altitude. On a better day I'd have gone closer to the terrain and used the lift from the cloud to fly fast along this face, but today my strategy was simple – stay away from anything hard. That included the ground and particularly the jagged, pointy mountains. In fact I was probably more than a kilometre away from them all the time.

This seemed to be going rather well, but I was still concerned. A lifting line won't go on for ever, and what goes up has to come down somewhere. I was making progress but I needed to ensure I found somewhere safe to land. Importantly, it could not be in this valley. There was about 25km of valley to fly through and on an ordinary day landing along it would have been possible, but the landing options were few and far between as the valley was very built up with houses and the rest was full of trees. More importantly it became quite narrow and the wind was clearly funnelling through it. If it was windy where I was, at 2500m, then it would be howling down there. Scared of the situation, I started circling in an extremely weak patch of lift in the middle of the valley. The wind was so strong that going round in circles was taking me in the direction I wanted to go at nearly 40km/h so it seemed like a smart thing to do – stay circling and maintain the height whilst getting drifted down the valley. When the zeros turned into sink I left on a glide again, expecting to have similar air than before but it wasn't to be. I was going downwind at nearly 80km/h but the sinking air I was in was so severe that my instruments were telling me at one point that I had a glide angle of 3:1! I was literally falling out of the sky! I even looked up at my wing to check I wasn't in a parachutal stall! Looking at the town, the trees, the wires and the narrow river gorge below me, I began to shudder inside. There was little that I could do but hold the glider steady through the turbulence and hope I came out the other side into better air before I was so low that I'd have to pick a tree to crash into. Luckily, the sinking air was short lived and I came out the other side of it with a reasonable amount of height into more normal air. Now I knew I'd make it over Chiavenna and this was my ticket out of here.

Thomas had turned south at this point and flown the ten kilometres or so to the top of Lake Como. I could easily have done the same but I had other plans. Immediately to the west of Chiavenna a line of mountains runs north-south. Heading south now would just lead me to a point where the mountains were wider and crossing by foot would take much longer. Instead, my plan was to cross at the Forcola pass which connects back over into Switzerland to the west. This had been my intention even before I had launched. The problem was the pass was at 2300m and there was no way in the world I was going to attempt to fly over it in these conditions. The valley floor here is very low indeed, only around 200m, and the slopes are steep, but I'd walked over the pass on a wet day of training in June. There were some open fields on a shoulder at about 1500m, but even that looked optimistic: I was only about 1200m as I came round the corner and just as Thomas had warned me, the wind was horrific here. As well as blowing down the valley I'd just flown down, it was also funnelling down through the Splügen pass to the north. The two winds were meeting here and having one hell of an argument! Trying to stay positive, I noted that after Chiavenna, where the valley turned south, it also opened out into a wide valley with many large open fields. This is where I needed to land. With all that in mind I flew into the middle of the valley, still 1000m above the deck, parked my glider into wind facing north, and more or less level with the starting point for the walk up the Forcola pass. If it would have been just a matter of sitting into wind and letting the height slowly decrease until I landed it would have been easy. The reality was quite different. I picked a field quite early on, it was long and thin, and I tried to line up with the upwind end of it. I couldn't stay over it without the speed bar on, even at altitude the wind was stronger than my trim speed. When I pushed the speed bar I struggled to keep the glider stable in the turbulent air. I was being thrown around like a bag of washing. At one point I connected with a ripping thermal, instinctively I hooked into it and the vario sang as I climbed at 3m/s, but despite the relative tranquillity inside the thermal, to take the climb would be madness, I was already losing ground fast and the urge to get on the ground overcame my natural piloting instincts once again. On the west side of the valley where the path wound its way up to the Forcola pass the trees were literally thrashing around. Even if I had been high enough there would have been no way I'd have been landing up there.

After what seemed like an age the ground came close enough to start thinking through my landing strategy. Despite my best efforts, the wind had pushed me south and the kilometre long field that I'd wanted to get into was out of reach upwind of me. I'd been reasonably smart and kept a big area of open fields behind me, and now I was letting myself be blown back despite it taking me further away from where I wanted to be. Frankly I didn't care as long as I got out of this one safely. The open fields behind me were criss-crossed with cables and power lines, which made the approach even more challenging than it already was. I found a gap and lined myself up. By now, close to the ground, I was going backwards extremely fast, about 15km/h (which, given the trim speed of the glider meant that the wind must have been around 55km/h). Anyone who has landed backwards on a paraglider will tell you it is extremely hard to do at this speed, you quite literally have to strain your neck to see where you are going, whilst at the same time trying to keep the wing inflated and above you! Finally, I touched down, let my knees bend and then hauled the wing to the ground as quickly as I could before I turned into a land surfer being dragged across the fields behind a flapping paraglider. With adrenalin coursing through my veins, I packed quickly, sheltered from the wind behind a very pretty little chalet. I needed to pee desperately but this person's nice house was not an appropriate place, so I shouldered my pack and headed for the main road to walk back across the several kilometres of terrain I'd just been blown downwind across. As I emerged by the main road there was a small building which turned out to be a public toilet, not only that but it was a very clean toilet with running water and soap. Amazing, just what I needed and just where I needed it. I stuck my head under the tap (it was hot down here at these low altitudes) and suddenly I was laughing out loud, I'd just cheated death once again and I felt on top of the world!

On that flight I'd crossed back into Italy. It seemed that I couldn't shake off this country quite yet.

I'd more or less flown 35km in a straight line at speeds of up to 80km/h. Dad meanwhile had to walk back down the hill and then drive along winding mountain roads, probably for about double that distance, in order to catch up with me. By the time he did catch up with me, I'd walked some way, almost to the point where I'd need to leave the roads to walk up the mountain again.

I was feeling pretty relaxed now. I was confident that the route over the Forcola pass was the most efficient one, and

I had plenty of time. I wouldn't make it up there tonight and in any case the wind was still so strong that flying wouldn't be possible. No, the plan was rather to make it to the top tomorrow morning at first light and fly down the other side in the direction of Bellinzona in the early morning smooth air. So although it was now only late afternoon I'd only need to walk up to the highest point that the mountain tracks would allow us to get the van to and sleep there for the night. That point was about 1300m up the mountain above the tiny hamlets of Foppo and Voga. Once again, our preparation paid off as we knew exactly where to go and where we could get the van up to.

Although there was a road up here, it was a single track affair that hair-pinned back and forwards. There was also a much older paved path, dating from a time before motor vehicles and this route was pretty direct. It was in the shade of the forest and springs and shrines to the Virgin Mary littered the route. The springs were welcome as I didn't need to carry water, but the shrines, so obviously necessary to an earlier generation who must have used this route regularly, seemed rather redundant, at least for my heathen needs. As it was still early we decided for once not to stop for food and then push on further but rather get to our final resting place high up on the mountain slopes and have dinner there. It was still light when I reached it, so I sat in the last of the evening sunshine and relaxed. A good meal eaten slowly, some housekeeping completed and soon darkness began to fall on our little van perched up on the mountainside. The lights started to twinkle in the valley far, far below us. It seemed strange to think I'd landed down there just this afternoon, it felt like a different world already, somehow disconnected from our reality. In a strange way, I felt like I was on holiday rather than in the middle of the world's most extreme race!

One thing bothered me though. The wind will normally ease off as the darkness falls, but instead the wind was still blowing rather strongly down the pass. I was worried for the

morning – the wind was the one thing that could scupper my
cunning plan.

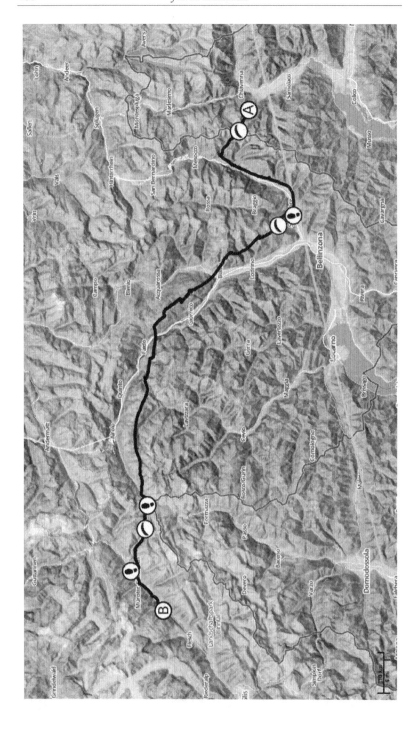

Day 9: Forcola to Blitzingen

3.30am feels awfully early. I was up and getting food inside me, ready to start walking at 4am, the time when the compulsory rest period finished. Even with a 4am start I'd only make the top an hour or so after sunrise, as I still had a thousand metres to climb. I stepped out of the van to the one noise I did not want to hear – the trees rustling in the wind. The wind was still blowing down from the pass as it had the night before and I was pretty sure that if there was a steady 10 km/h of wind here blowing down the slope then a thousand metres above me, in the narrow gap that formed the Forcola pass, there would be a gale blowing. Still, I was committed to this route now, so as the clock ticked 4am, I shouldered my pack and headed up the mountain by the light of my head torch, glad to have already walked this path in training.

On the way up I'd convinced myself it would not be flyable, but two hours later as I came over the pass I was relieved to find that the wind was not blowing too fiercely through the gap. There was some wind, but only about 15-20 km/h. I decided I'd be fine as I wolfed down a banana at the col. The wind aloft was still northerly, consistent with the forecast, so I started to contour round on the south side expecting the wind to be coming more up the slope on this side of the pass, and therefore offering a suitable site to launch from. As I started to do so it became apparent that the wind was actually coming more from the south. This was rather odd. Luckily though there was a hump that allowed me to take off more or less facing into the wind, and from here I could glide across to the north side and fly the south facing cliffs out towards the main valley, still about 7km to my west. I picked the wing up in smooth steady wind and glided across to the cliffs, where, as expected from the wind direction I'd experienced at the launch point, I joined smooth lifting air. Suddenly I was in a different world, I was climbing in perfectly smooth lift at a rate of 1.8m/s (which is pretty damn quick!). I was soaring along beautiful cliffs in the early morning sunshine. I was loving it, it felt too good to be true. Realising that the length of my flight would be dependent on the height I gained here I turned around facing back towards the col and started another 'beat' along the cliffs, still screaming upwards in this incredible ridge lift. The cliffs here actually dropped towards the col and soon I was soaring up towards the crest. I always find it a special moment when I climb up past a jagged mountain edge, one minute close to the cliffs, the next clear air all around. It is a most exhilarating feeling and, for me, one of the experiences that most sums up why I go paragliding. To be doing this in ridge lift at 6.30am felt surreal, almost wrong. It was wrong.

My world fell apart, it came crashing around me. One second I was invincible in sublime ridge lift and the next I was fighting to keep the wing inflated above me. I was being tossed around like a piece of flotsam in a mountain stream. I couldn't think, all I could do was hang on to the wing and point away from the cliffs. My self-preservation instinct told me to get out of there pretty damn quick. I was heading away from the cliff now and still being hurled around, but to add to my issues I was now falling out of the sky – I was in extremely strongly sinking air, my instruments told me I was doing over 3m/s down and I had a head wind to push against to get out of this high valley. I was flying west now, towards the main valley, and watched with disbelief as my glide looked like it wasn't even going to be enough to escape the valley. Below me were only trees. There was one option to land in half way down, near a flat plateau with a little house, but if I put the wing down here I'd be walking the rest of it as I knew there was nowhere to launch on the other side of this plateau. A panic was welling up inside me as I clung on the rear risers, speed bar pushed as much as I dare to try to get out of this horrid place. Once again I'd gone from hero to zero in a few short moments! That short glide seemed to take forever; my whole body was tense with effort and fear. Finally after what seemed like an age, the sink abated, and I knew I'd make it out of this valley now.

As my side valley joined the main valley, I cut the corner to find myself in an area of convergence, the wind was blowing down the main valley from the north here. Suddenly I felt like a fool. It was obvious now what had been happening, I was just too stupid, too tired or to occupied with keeping the wing flying to have realised it earlier. The wind was coming strongly from the north and so the valley I launched in was sheltered by the cliffs, the southerly direction in the wind I felt when I launched was because the wind was rotoring over the cliffs and the whole valley was like a great washing machine of wind, like a horizontal whirlpool. The lovely ridge lift had in fact been the updraft from the wind rotoring over the top. I felt stupid because if I'd realised this earlier I could have just kept on the north side of the valley and surfed the roll over all the way into the main valley, leaving before the ridge line dropped to my height to scoot away across the valley. Even after the horrific experience where I hit the shear layer I could have turned back out of the sink to the north side once again and had an easy ride out of the valley, but instead I stayed in the middle, right at the point the wind was flushing down. I was annoyed with myself for not having worked this out earlier, but then again, I don't normally fly paragliders in the big mountains in strong wind at 6.30am, so these aren't the types of situations I normally have to figure out when I am flying!

Determined to make up for my earlier errors, I climbed in the convergence lift that I now found myself in, working hard to circle in the rough air. A large bird of prey above me was also taking the benefit of this lift to climb, and I used him as a marker to keep myself in the best air. The north wind meant I kept having to push north to stay in the right place, but gradually I climbed several hundred meters back up. I looked up once again to my feathered companion only to see him thrown violently to one side and seemingly dive out of something. It was my turn next. Half the wing folded under as I hit the same air. I didn't need a second telling – it was time to get out of here! I set of south down the main valley, stopping and turning into wind at the next spur to take advantage of the lift where the valley wind was hitting the spur. My ground speed went to zero. I swore to myself: that means 40km/h of wind in the valley blowing down from the north, I knew it had been strong but I wasn't really able to feel how strong earlier in the area of convergence. Now I was out of that and in the full flow of the wind howling down from the Bernadino pass. At least the flying was easy and predictable now, I hopped from spur to spur, turning into wind at each spur and taking a bit of lift parked into the wind, before turning and diving downwind again. It wasn't enough to keep me high, but it was enough to keep me heading south towards Bellinzona.

And then, something strange happened. As the valley started to open out near Roveredo, the valley wind disappeared. I don't mean it was lighter, I mean, gone, nothing. As the valley turned round to the west I skimmed across a mountain face that should have had the wind flowing up it on the outside of the valley bend, but there was nothing, the trees were not even fluttering. It seemed remarkable a few kilometres back I had a 40km/h wind and now there was no wind, but, with hindsight, the only explanation is that the wind from the north was pushed up over a different air mass that was stable in the bottom of this low valley, I must have dropped out of the upper layer where the wind was no doubt still blowing (all that air has to go somewhere, right?).

After an adrenalin-filled flight which had me on full concentration the whole time, I was now gliding in clear smooth morning air, heading for the middle of the valley and a disused airfield. I was relaxed. Very relaxed. Suddenly waves of tiredness washed over me and warm mellow thoughts started to swim around in my head. I was gliding holding on to the risers with my feet out horizontally resting against the foot plate of my pod harness. My eyes started to feel heavy and I figured I could rest them for a while. I woke briefly as my hands slipped down off of the risers, but it wasn't enough, I couldn't fight the tiredness.

Next thing I knew I awoke with a start as my legs dropped below me, no longer able to stay straight as my whole body had started to give in to the sleep. This time it was enough, I was only a few hundred feet up and I needed to get on to the ground. I was awake and alert again, shocked with myself that I'd just briefly fallen asleep in mid-air. Now I came gliding into a small field next to the airfield (the airfield itself was surrounded by a rather large fence so I figured landing in it wouldn't be too smart in case there was no way out). I turned and flew over a lady walking her dog and landed a few meters further on. It was still early, only just past 7am. As I was climbing out of my harness the lady caught up with me and said something to me in Italian. Despite not speaking any Italian I surprised myself by understanding what she had said. Even so I couldn't respond in her tongue so I said politely in English that I was English and didn't speak Italian. She repeated her remark in excellent English. She basically said "Cold isn't it?" Little did I know then how relevant those words would turn out to be. She was absolutely right, at only 300m altitude in mid-July, it was surely not normal to have to wear a thick winter coat to walk your dog.

I packed quickly and after a brief strategy check I decided to head up the mountain right next to me. It was going to be a good flying day and I needed to be in a good place to launch by mid-morning. The trouble was that to get to where I needed to launch I'd need to climb over 2000 vertical metres. This was because the slopes here were completely tree covered to that height, as I'd discovered searching for launch sites here in training. I had the option to continue towards Lugano, giving me a longer walk on the flat but with a climb to a take-off at about 1300m. I estimated that this would take slightly longer and put me in more challenging starting place, and one that I didn't know, not having flown there in practice. I was also pleased to find that my choice of coming over the Forcola pass was vindicated. I'd just landed more or less level with Thomas and Ferdy who were walking along the valley to the south of me. Between the 3 of us we were more or less level pegging for 4th place. What's more I'd achieved this with relatively little walking; my scary flight had paid out! I'd just managed to fly about 24km before 7.30am!

The section of the route from this point until the next turn point at the Matterhorn offered the most diverse choice of routes of any part of the course. For me there were essentially two options, the direct line, passing precariously along the northern edge of, and then under, Lugano airspace, or north up the Leventina valley and over the Nuefenen pass. For those behind who were already further south than I was there was another option to the south of Lugano airspace, taking a more or less direct line towards the turn point. The challenge for the guys taking the direct line was that, on approaching the Matterhorn from the east you had to either walk up over the Monte Rosa glacier (3500m and requiring a mountain guide and full mountaineering gear) or cross via the Simplon pass. I'd ruled out the glacier option, because the forecast indicated that it may not be possible to fly down the other side – if this would be the case it would take a very long time negotiating the descent by foot. For me it simply was not worth the risk. I still had the option of the south route with the crossing at the Simplon Pass. I decided to leave the decision until I was in the air – it would be a flying day so I'd let the flying conditions dictate my choice.

Walking up out of the valley from the small village of San Vittore I started to make some calls. Ali, my wife was rather worried as she told me there was an airfield marked on the map close to where I'd landed. She was concerned because if there had been restricted airspace around it then it would have meant a penalty or disqualification. I told her, yes, indeed I was aware there was an airfield there as I'd landed right next to it, but reassured her there was no restricted airspace there. Next call was to Dad, who was still some way off but I gave him directions to meet me about half way up the mountain where the footpath I was walking on passed a small road accessing some chalets perched on this hillside. He was still some way off, despite the 4am start, as he had had probably the most epic drive of the whole race: there is no road that crosses the line of mountains I'd just come across. His only way to get to me was to first drive back east down the mountain we'd been on, then head a long way north, over the Splügen pass, then turn west and drive up and over the Bernadino pass before finally driving south down the valley I'd just be blown along. It was several hundred kilometres of windy mountain roads compared to my 24km flight!

The rendezvous worked, although I still made it there before him (albeit only by a minute or so). I'd left my glider in the big lay-by exactly where the footpath crossed the road, and disappeared behind a log pile to relieve myself. While I was there Dad pulled up in the van but rather than stopping right next to the bag (which was the whole point of me leaving it there) he stopped 30m further up the road. Now, it probably sounds ridiculous, given I'd already climbed over 2000m that morning and had covered a lot of kilometres by foot, but I was grumpy about having to walk an unnecessary 30m. I walked across to my bag, Dad had stepped out of the van by now, and I shouted to him, in as good natured a voice as I could muster, 'why did you stop all the way up there?' I pulled myself together and decided there was no reason to fall out over such a silly thing and I walked, without bag, up to the van. The bag could stay there and I'd pick it up when I set off again.

A hearty meal, fresh clothes and an equipment reshuffle later (no need for the head torch I still had with me, for example) and I was off again walking up the mountain. The path took me through a dense pine forest, and I was amazed to see thousands of ants under my feet more or less the whole way up. There were huge ants' nests by the path and the creatures made the path almost look black in places. I became obsessed with how many ants there must be. I tried to estimate how many were on each square foot of path and then multiply it up, but the numbers were too big and it made my mind boggle. I wondered if there were more ants in the world than humans, and decided there must be. It then occurred to me that from afar we humans must look like this too, packed into cities, whole areas literally swarming with people. The whole ant/human analogy was starting to make me think that I'd spent too much time walking with my brain churning over things (maybe Nietszche was right after all).

Finally I emerged from the trees and scrambled up a boulder field before arriving on a ridge with a grassy slope that I could launch from. There were already good clouds above me and I was in a hurry to get airborne. I quickly dressed into warm clothes, including my thick down jacket, and launched into good air. After a couple of minutes I knew I'd made a clothing mistake. It was cold in the air and my down jacket was next to useless because I'd forgotten to bring my windproof layer to go over the top of it. Without the wind proof layer the wind was just going straight through my clothes. I was already starting to shiver and I wasn't even high yet. I climbed a bit and then headed north towards better looking clouds but frustratingly it was weak here and I had to turn and fly back to my take off point to find a better climb. Eventually connecting with a good strong thermal, I started to climb out. All of a sudden there was a bang and I knew instantly something had broken, I quickly checked the glider, all was fine. I then realised that my harness felt wrong and I worked out that a line supporting the foot plate on the left side had broken. This was not an auspicious start to the flight – I'd only just launched and I was already cold with a broken harness!

Reaching cloud base, it was decision time. The crossing towards Lugano was not so far but I knew low down in the valley the wind would be against me and I was not as high as I'd have liked. So, I headed north. It was not so much a great tactical decision, rather more of a spontaneous choice driven by not wanting to cross the valley at this point. But it meant I was now committed to the route via the Nuefenen pass. It also meant that for the next 20km or so I would be heading almost due north, at right angles to the course line (as one commentator who was following the live tracking would comment, 'where the hell are you going, England?') Well, I wasn't heading to England but compared to all the other little coloured lines all heading west my light blue line heading north must have looked rather odd. A close friend remembers looking at the tracking at that point and thinking, 'I hope he has a plan'!

The flying for the first 10km was straight forward, heading along a line of mountains I only had to turn a few times, staying close to cloud base. But after that there was a short transition over the town of Biasca. The ridge beyond had a great big towering cumulus, but high cloud was coming over and the big cumulus was obviously decaying. Clouds build when thermals feed them, but once these thermals stop the clouds gradually decay.

A decaying cloud was a bad sign, particularly one this big as it was blocking the sun. I had no choice though, and I pushed on aware that I needed to switch my flying style from fast, only turning in the strongest climbs, to just staying up, circling in anything until the sun came out and proper thermals started again. My judgement was right this time and I spent some time on the next hill staying more or less the same height, climbing in weak bubbles and then pushing on and climbing again, using every bit of lift to stay up. I was managing to stay level with the top of the ridge, but only just. At least the air was a little warmer down here! Finally my patience paid off and, at the north end someone flicked the magic thermal switch back on and I was able to climb easily back to cloud base.

I had not been able to see much to the north due to the large cloud here but now, as I came out from under it I could see properly. The ridge line dropped back from the valley and it would be a long glide into the back of this bowl. At the same time there was one great big cloud that was rather too smooth at the top. I couldn't quite get my head round it all but it just didn't feel right. I normally fly on data, making conscious choices based on what I understand around me. This time it was just instinct, it felt wrong so I turned left and glided across the valley. I honestly can't explain why I did it, I just did! Half way across I started to question my decision. What on earth was I doing leaving the south west faces of the valley on a great flying day to glide into the north facing side of the valley? Suddenly it seemed like madness, but I was committed now.

I was in strong sink crossing the valley and the options on the other side didn't look great. I started thinking negatively and found myself looking at the valley for landing options, working out the position of the road and the best side to end up on to continue the walk towards the Nuefenen pass. What on earth was I doing? I gave myself a mental kick up the arse and made myself start trying to figure out where I'd be able to climb on the other side of the valley. Despite the north east faces, there was a tree covered knoll, and the valley wind would be blowing onto it. I decided this would be my best bet. As I came over the knoll I found a weak climb which I worked carefully, patiently gaining the height I'd need to glide across to a ridge to my north. Finally, I dropped back onto the ridge and started working a better climb as I drifted over a small lake and a cable care station perched high up on the mountain. The views were stunning and I was beginning to relax. Crossing to this side of the valley had been the right decision after all. In front of me there was an amazing cloud street running due west whereas the other side there seemed to be some type of wave effect. A sailplane joined my climb above me. I was now within reach of the start of the cloud street but I was still cautious, if I went on a glide now and it didn't work out I'd end up dropping back into the valley onto the north faces, whereas once I connected with the cloud street I'd be able to cruise along above the rocky spines feeding this mass of rising air. The sailplane left heading in the direction I wanted to go. I watched him go and there was no strong sink on the short transition, and sure enough he started to climb strongly as he connected underneath the cloud street. To my amazement he started circling, which seemed unnecessary to me! Nevertheless, I followed, reassured.

The next section of this flight was pure exhilaration and pure torture at the same time. The exhilaration came because the cloud base was at 3300m and the lift was strong, so I was just flying in a straight line, speed bar on, holding the glider as steady as I could through the bumpy bits. The views to the south into the Maglia valley were stunning, as was the view ahead to the Nuefenen pass and to the north towards the Furka pass. Small lakes dotted the high mountains and the rocky summits glowed in the sunshine. It was amazing, but it was torture because I was excruciatingly cold. I'd long since lost the feeling in my hands. The icy wind cut straight through my clothing: I might as well have been wearing nothing, that's what it felt like. My body seemed to be shutting down from the cold and it was all I could do to keep the speed bar pushed. The cold even seemed to be numbing my brain as I struggled to think about the next part of the flight. That Italian lady with the dog had been right. It was cold.

I followed the cloud street for 12km, but the sky was filling in very quickly. Clouds were developing everywhere that there was sunshine. By the time I reached the end there was almost total cloud cover, with very little sun left. I looked around and saw that the south facing cliffs just before the Nuefenen pass on the other side of the valley were still in the sun. I decided to cross the valley, figuring the cliffs would still be working and in any case I only needed a little bit of lift to squeeze through the pass. The conditions would be better on the other side in the Goms valley, they always are!

I only realised too late that it was an error. This north wind was pushing over the 3000m peaks on the other side of the valley and flushing down the faces. The reason they were still in sun was because the air was sinking here and preventing any clouds forming. It was the strong head wind that I was pushing against half way across that made me realise all this, but it was too late, all I could do was push the speed bar and try to make as much progress up the valley towards the Nuefenen Pass as I could. With hindsight I could have tried to stay on the south side of the valley, but everything was completely grey on that side and the clouds tracked back away into remote high altitude terrain, with no access. On a good flying day with sun it would have been a good route choice but it would have been a high risk choice on this day.

I landed next to the road, and with numb hands struggled to unclip myself from the harness. I sat on my haunches, arms wrapped around my knees hugging myself and gently rocking backwards and forwards in a desperate attempt to warm up. It took 5 minutes before I was able to move properly and even then I was in agony. As the blood flowed into my extremities the nerves screamed back, racking my body with excruciating 'hot aches'. Having seen me at over 3000m before the Nuefenen Pass Dad had wrongly assumed that I would easily cross the pass and was merrily driving down the other side of it when I called him back by phone. I needed a hot drink and some psychological support. I was in a bit of a state, I was very hungry and my body was rebelling after having to endure such extreme cold. Still I'd managed to land at nearly 2000m so for once I only had 500m to climb to get over the next high mountain pass.

By now I was really beginning to appreciate all the people following my race online and I knew many people would find it rather odd to have seen me suddenly fly out into the valley and land, particularly because it is always sunny on Google Earth! So I took a picture of the rather foreboding dark grey sky and posted to the website from my phone as a diary entry, with the simple caption, 'sky at the Nuefenen Pass for all those following on live tracking'.

Walking once again, I took the typical short cuts to avoid the hairpin bends and came across a whole herd of mountain chamois nonchalantly wandering about on the road near to the top.

Arriving at the top of what Dad had taken to calling the Nurofen Pass, I had to stop. I needed to take a break and eat some food. Even though the wind was not too strong and it was possible to launch here, I really couldn't go on, so there was no choice. It was a shame though, as there may have been a chance to get out and down the Goms valley if I'd launched earlier from here. To be honest, I had not even expected to be able to launch from the Nuefenen pass at all because I'd expected the wind to be too strong. So after a huge bowl of pasta I walked over the lip of the pass in front of the main car park and took off once more. I was only expecting a glide to the valley, but obviously I was going to do my best to stay up and keep flying if I could. The SW face was all in shade as I set off on my glide. As it was now getting late in the afternoon I decided to glide out along the NE face, because this would pick up that famous north wind blowing down the valley. Out towards the main Goms valley I managed to find a weak climb on the corner and stayed with it for what seemed like forever, circling scarily close to massive power lines. At this point I noticed the SW face I'd ignored was now in the sun and had a nice cloud over it and probably would have been the better option. I was too belligerent to go back to it. I was expecting the south side of the valley (so the NW faces) to be at least buoyant, meaning I'd be able to fly along it without losing too much height. The lift on the corner I'd been circling in indicated this might be the case so I set off down the valley. The problem here was that there is a gliding club in the valley and there is a surprisingly large area of restricted airspace around it. If I lost too much height I'd end up in the restricted zone. With only trees on the slope below me landing wouldn't be an option either. It was immediately apparent I did not stand a chance of squeezing past the airspace on this side, as I started to loose height, so I turned back and flew across the valley to the SE facing slopes, but I was too low to connect to anything there either and so found myself screaming at the stupid airspace, essentially stuck against a virtual wall that I could not pass. I spiralled off the height and landed as close to the airspace as I dared.

Now all I could do was walk down the road which descends this beautifully desolate valley. After a few kilometres I saw, on my left, the tarmac strip of the runway that was the very reason I was on the ground here and not at least 5 kilometres further on. I was quite surprised how steeply the valley was dropping when I noticed a road ahead of me that contoured along the hillside. The vertical distance between the road and the valley floor increased as the valley floor dropped away. I could see some open fields a few kilometres further on that would be launchable and I started thinking. With a steeply sloping valley and a slight tail wind, I would not need to be very far above the valley floor to be able to get quite a distance along. Hmmm. Dad pulled up in the van and we fished out the maps and the airspace diagram – the issue was that I was still in the restricted airspace and I could not tell if the fields I could see in the distance, next to the road that contoured along the valley side, were still inside or outside the airspace. This was not easy to work out as we were trying to correlate information from various different maps of different scales. It was at this point two guys from the sailplane club found us and came to say hello. They were genuinely friendly but we were focussed on trying to work out if flying was an option and to be blunt they were simply a distraction. But then I figured they knew the area pretty well so I quickly explained what I was planning and the issue with the airspace that we were trying to figure out. One of them looked at me with a slightly shocked expression and said to me to be careful because, 'there aren't many places to land in this valley between here and Fiesch'. I was dumbstruck for a moment – the Goms valley is wide and completely devoid of trees on the valley floor, although the fields do undulate at odd angles created by great glacial deposits where side valleys seem to literally spill out into the main valley. Then it dawned on me – they were sailplane pilots of course – landing a sailplane here could indeed be a handful, but for a paraglider it was no issue at all. I rather uncharitably looked at them and through clenched teeth said, 'trust me, I can land *anywhere* between here and Fiesch'. Finally, and reluctantly, we concluded that the possible take off spots would still be inside the airspace and I resigned myself to walking along the road for the next couple of hours until our dinner stop.

I was now past the airspace and feeling uneasy about walking down this valley, it seemed I was just wasting precious altitude. So, flushed with the success of this morning's start, we hatched a plan to end today as we'd ended yesterday. I'd walk up the side of the valley heading up the mountain until we ran out of road and then we'd stop there for the night – I could then continue up the rest in the morning, for an early flight to hop along the valley.

As a rule, I did not pay too much attention to the positions on the live tracking. The people who had flown the south route were close to the turn point whilst I was stopping for the night still a long way out. Logic told me I was in a much better position than my ranking suggested as I now had a pretty clear run into Zermatt along the valleys, whilst many of the others had a 3500m glacier to cross tomorrow morning. Still, I found myself questioning my choice, wondering if this had been a dumb route after all. Logic was one thing, but emotion was fighting to take control. I doubted myself and despondency was eating away at me. Thank goodness I had people supporting me who believed in me and who reassured me, but it is a measure of my state that I wondered to myself if they were just telling me I was in a good position to make me feel better. A part of me speculated that maybe they thought I'd mucked up by choosing the Nuefenen route. And so I finished the day doubting myself but at the same time determined to make tomorrow count.

Day 10: Blitzingen to St Niklaus (via the Matterhorn)

Ten days into this race and I'd have thought any hike up a mountain would be fine. After the technical ascent of the Dachstein by via ferrata on day 2 or the long painful drag up the Stelvio pass a few days earlier, a relatively short ascent up a predominantly grassy slope should have been easy. It turned out not to be. The first part was fine, leaving the van more or less at first light, but as I got higher the path petered out until I was walking across an open hillside. Whichever line I took it turned out to be the wrong one. One minute I was traipsing through boggy ground, the mud seemingly sucking my sodden feet back to the ground and making every step harder, the next I was scrambling over unfeasibly large boulders. At times a myriad of tiny rivers made it seem like I was forever picking my way across water courses. All this meant the going was frustratingly slow. Furthermore the steep sides of the Goms valley seemed to have flattened out at just the point I wanted to launch.

My plan was a simple one. The day was good, early morning sunshine and no wind. I needed to get enough height here to glide across the valley and land on the slopes below the paragliding take off at Fiesch. This was a SE facing site and it would work very early. Today the weather would be good to start with but the day would quickly overdevelop and the opportunity to fly would be limited to the morning. I was, by luck, in about the best place possible to take advantage of this weather.

Back on my tussock covered hillside I felt as though I was back in Cumbria or Wales and not in the mighty Alps. To my left, I could see a good part of the slope to launch from that was just round the corner of a spur and would be facing across the valley I needed to glide over. This is the valley where the Fiesch glacier spills out into the main valley. By climbing here and gliding across I was saving myself the tedious walk down the valley to Fiesch, which would have cost me 300m in altitude, instead I'd be able to glide that and would only have a short walk back up on the other side, having saved myself five kilometres of walking to boot.

The challenge was to get the balance right. I needed enough height to connect with the open slopes around the Fiesch launch, where I could land and wait for the thermals to start. If I came in too low the slopes were forested and landing would be a challenge. On the other hand, I didn't want to walk up any further than absolutely necessary. I'd calculated I needed to be at about 2400m, and I had finally reached that magic height. I'd have liked to have taken a little more height to be sure, but the ground flattened out here and it would have been a long walk to gain a few extra meters, so trusting my arithmetic I started preparing to launch.

Unlike most of my flights over the last couple of days, this one was going to be an early morning glide in still air. What is more the take-off was perfect, a grass slope at the perfect angle for a nil wind forward launch, my only witnesses were rather a lot of sheep that seemed mightily grumpy about this great white crinkly thing disturbing their early morning munching.

On flights like this there is actually nothing to do as a pilot. Once in the air I simply had to point the wing at the slopes opposite me across this side valley, tuck my hands behind the risers, point my toes and generally try to be as aerodynamic as possible. Apart from that all I could do was watch the numbers on my instruments, which tell me altitude, glide ratio and sink rate. They did not make very good reading. I watched the altitude drop away quicker than it should have done in still air. Nothing alarming, I was gliding hands off in perfectly calm air, but air that was obviously descending enough to throw my calculations. All I could do was hope. No matter how much I tried to recalculate in my head the numbers didn't get better. It reminded me of when I started flying competitions in the 1990's and we'd calculate the final glides manually. In those days I'd recalculate the final glide to goal over and over in my head, checking my altitude and the distance on the map and recalculating if I was going to make it or not. It gave my something to focus on as well as making sure I stayed on track. These days of course this isn't necessary as modern instruments calculate the final glide for us.

Ahead of me on the approaching hillside, the tree line dipped down to accommodate the bottom station of a chair lift. This was the point I was aiming for, hoping to scrape in over the trees and land next to the chair lift. As I came closer though it was clear it wasn't to be. Luckily for me, below the tree line there was a gap that looked like it may be a ski slope down into the valley in the winter. It was quite narrow and pretty steep, but it provided what I needed – the chance to land up here. Frustratingly though I now had the opposite problem, I was too high to land at the highest point on this open sliver of land, so I had to put in two circles to lose some more height in order to squeeze the glider into the gap.

It was still early and I was feeling pretty confident of my plan now. All I needed to do was pack and walk about 400m up the hillside to the take-off above me. Clouds were already growing in the Goms valley, back in the direction I'd come from. Clearly the day was going to start soon, and this time, unlike in the Dolomites, I was ready for it.

As is only too common in ski resorts in the summer, great bulldozers were working on the slopes above me, landscaping the ski runs so we can all enjoy our controlled descent through the unspoilt snow covered slopes. Unfortunately, most of the slopes we all ski on are far from unspoilt under that pristine carpet of snow; they are bulldozed and shaped by machinery, leaving great scars on the mountains. My concern on this day though was not about the state of the mountainside. The problem with the bulldozers was that I was walking straight up the slope below them and every now and then great lumps of rock dislodged by them would come rolling down the slope. It wasn't that steep so not overly alarming, but as I came closer I did make sure I was not directly below the noise of their thundering diesel engines.

Finally I came level with the take-off and I could see half a dozen wings laid out on the launch, still a hundred meters or so away across the slope. As I reached the take-off I dropped my bag and was slightly surprised that no one greeted me. Throughout the race I'd been met by pilots almost wherever I went, people following me on live tracking and coming out to walk with me, or just coming to say 'hi' whilst I stopped for food. Now here I was about to launch from a proper paraglider take-off (for the first time since the Gaisberg on the first day, incidentally!), it was full of pilots and not one of them even took a look at this exhausted guy dressed in race clothing and covered in logos...odd.

I pulled my wing out of the bag and laid out behind everyone, it was still very early and these were all clearly low airtime pilots getting ready for a flight down. Still nothing. Even with my wing out and 'Red Bull X-Alps' written across it in half meter high letters, no one said a thing. It was not that I wanted the attention, in fact I prefer not to be the centre of attention, I'd rather just quietly get on and do my own thing, but still it was beginning to become unsettling.

Finally the obvious dawned on me. This was a

paragliding school – they all hooked up their radios and the instructor was checking the radio connection and that they were clipped in properly before she let each one of them launch. They probably had never even heard of the X-Alps!

I went across to the instructor and introduced myself. Even though I'd flown here many times, local knowledge is invaluable, especially from someone who is chucking people off this mountain early in the morning every day. As I told her I was in the X-Alps she rather nonchalantly remarked 'I thought so, when I saw you walking up'. Even though it was only 9am, we talked about the weather for the day, she confirmed that it would overdevelop and probably close in (meaning total cloud cover) but that storms were unlikely here. She also confirmed that it started working very early here. The fact that about half her students had actually gone up on their glides out from the hill, meant there was clearly lifting air but it was weak. Still she reassured me that it works much earlier than most people think. With a big and rather moist cloud only 200m above the take-off it looked like indeed it was already working. But the question was: do I take the risk? I didn't want to blow it too early but at the same time the flying window was also looking like it would be frustratingly short.

Once all her students were off, she offered to hang around a bit after launching herself, to show me how well (or not) it was actually working. It was about at this point, as my helpful (if rather understated) instructor friend was getting her own wing ready to launch that 3 pilots arrived from the cable car. They'd obviously seen on the live tracking that I was here and were ecstatic to find I hadn't yet launched. There followed a lot of picture taking and general celebration on their part. Normality had returned, but I wasn't sure it was an improvement!

With my instructor friend now in the air, it was clear that it was possible to maintain height in early morning climbs but there were no great thermals about. Still the clouds were growing and I needed to take my chances, so to the clicking of cameras from the newly arrived fan club, I took off. I climbed in some of the weakest air I have ever climbed in. It took forever, gliding out and then climbing back to launch height before losing it and sinking out again before climbing slowly and painstakingly back up. At times I was circling directly over the launch only 50 meters or so above it with the fan club waving to me. It probably took me about 25mins to get up to cloud base, which was only 200m above the take-off. Looking at my track log, those 200m took over 40 circles to climb! Next to the cloud the lift was a little stronger so I could finally set off south west in the direction of the Zermatt valley. This is a well flown route, probably one of the most famous paragliding highways in the alps. I knew where I was going. The low cloud made it hard work and I knew I did not want to lose much height given how weak the climbs were lower down. On the next spur I got the climb I needed to stay in the 'good zone' where the lift was stronger close to the cloud. This time it was a stronger thermal. I was able to climb a little higher as the stronger climb seemed to have pushed the cloud up. I needed every bit of height I could get though and I was taking every climb right up to the cloud, and then gliding out on a bearing if I momentarily lost sight of the ground.

Flying inside cloud is forbidden. It is against visual flight regulations which paragliders need to comply with. It was also a rule of the competition: any cloud flying would be penalised, at the discretion of the organisers. I don't fly in cloud. There are good reasons why it isn't allowed, and, more than anything else, in my opinion it is cheating. The frustrating thing was that some competitors were blatantly doing so and gaining big advantages from it. The problem for the organisers was that it is almost impossible to have clear evidence. Sometimes it is quite feasible to climb up the side of the cloud, so unless someone is actually seen to be in the cloud there seemed little that they were willing, or able, to do. So as I skimmed along the clouds heading south west from Fiesch, I did my best to tread the fine line between taking every climb as high as possible without ever circling into the cloud.

As I crossed over the end of the mighty Aletsch glacier, I started thinking about the crossing into the Zermatt valley. I had tried this twice before in training and both times I had not had enough height to climb on the other side and fly into the valley that would lead me to the Matterhorn. One thing was in my favour this time – it was earlier in the day and so the east faces should be working better and the valley wind should not be as ferocious as last time I'd tried it. Still there was one thing massively against me: altitude.

Climbing under a good cloud somewhere above Visp, still on the north side of the valley, I started to think I was a bit of a sucker. I started to convince myself that everyone else in this race was climbing into cloud when they needed to (in hindsight this was clearly unfair, whilst some were it certainly wasn't everyone). So why shouldn't I? As I circled up to a lovely cloud my climb rate started to increase rapidly from the weak climb I'd had in free air to the much stronger lift near to the cloud. I decided I'd climb into the cloud, I was a long way clear of the relief and it would get me across the valley. I let myself be engulfed and everything went white, I was banked over in my climb, vario singing away, this was it I thought, just hold on. But I couldn't do it. It just felt wrong. It was cheating and I did not want to cheat, so I rolled out of my climb and popped straight out of the cloud facing across the valley. I'd been tempted, I'd even tried it, but it was not how I wanted to run this race. I'd take whatever the Zermatt valley could throw at me from crossing at this height.

Gliding into the Zermatt valley was strange, I arrived just above the village of Zeneggen, perched high up on the east face of the mouth of the valley, as though standing guard for the town of Visp below. Above me there were clouds up on the rocky high slopes but I was pretty low, only at 1400m, and down here nothing much was working. I found some weak lift and circled hopefully but I could only squeeze a measly 50m or so from this pathetic climb. It was drifting me up the valley gently which was also odd, at this height I would have expected to be hurtling up the valley in a strong valley wind, but the wind was light. This was an indicator that there were not many thermals in the Zermatt valley today, for if there were then they'd be sucking the air in through this narrow gap and there'd be a much stronger wind here. I hung on a little longer, but it seemed pretty futile. I hoped that just a bit further round the corner, were the east slopes became rather more south-east facing slopes, that there would be a better chance of staying airborne. The problem was that around the corner the valley also got very narrow and rose steeply. There were also no reasonable landing options until St Niklaus, about 6km further on. I'd never had the guts to come in here low before, but with only a light valley breeze helping me along the valley it felt manageable and I figured something must be going up somewhere.

I was wrong. Nothing was going up. I thought I'd found a thermal close to the cliffs in a small gully, but after trying to gain some height there I realised it was in vain as it was only some very small and weak ridge lift caused by the gully scooping up the gentle breeze of the valley wind. A couple of hair-raisingly tight turns close to the cliff convinced me that at best I could maintain in this little bit of lift, but I wasn't going to be going up.

All I could do now was glide onwards towards St Niklaus. However, not for the first time in this race, I was without any landing options. Sometimes blind hope is the best policy, and besides there was nowhere to land in the other direction either, so I might as well continue in the direction I needed to go. Now the piloting skills were needed. Ahead of me I thought I could see an area that opened out a bit at the bottom of the valley. A railway clung to the right side of the valley and I could see a small road bridge across the stream. I started to think that perhaps I could land on the bridge. The problem was it would require pinpoint accuracy. As I came closer there appeared, like some kind of mirage, what looked like a field on the left side of the valley. Yes! It was a field… but closer still and I realised it was insanely steep and hemmed by trees up wind and downwind – it was tantalising but the approach would almost be impossible, except for a cross wind 'splat' type of landing. I was very low and running out of options now, but finally, at the last minute the solution presented itself. The minor road that crossed the river at the bottom of the valley dropped down from the main road on the east side. The slope it cut across was so steep that the tree tops from below the road did not come much above the height of the road itself. By turning into wind and lining myself up with this narrow single track road I could land easily on the road just at the point it crossed a small stream – this bridge was perfect as it meant that at that exact point there were no trees at all on the downslope side, just where I needed to touch down. Furthermore as the road was going uphill I was landing 'up slope' making it easy to land exactly on the spot I wanted to. I swung the glider round into wind and lined myself up with the road. Initially I kept a little way out from the slope, allowing me a view along the length of the road in order to see if there were any vehicles approaching. Luckily there were none, so I edged in to the slope, cleared the tree tops below the road and touched down exactly where I'd planned. In the end it all seemed to have been too easy.

As my feet connected with the road surface on the narrow bridge the wing stopped flying and started to float down towards me. As all the lines went slack I realised I'd focussed so much on the landing itself that I had not considered what would happen next. With the wing still above me but dropping to my left I started bunching the lines into my hands, as though I was gathering the wing up. It was an instinctive reaction to try to get the wing to me, but of course I could not do it quick enough, so I watched as the wing dropped to my left, the wrong side of the parapet of the bridge, and as though by magic entirely disappeared from my view. Luckily I had enough of the lines in my hand that it was now just suspended a few meters below hanging in free air below the bridge. I was also fortunate that this was a new bridge and so the 'parapet' was made of smooth metal. Carefully keeping hold of all the lines I peered over the edge. There didn't seem to be anything that could snag or tear the wing so I carefully hauled it back up onto the bridge. With my glider back safely in my hands and me safe on the ground I walked across to the verge and dumped my gear before I videoed the landing site for the diary. To this day, this has to be one of my all-time favourite landings on a paraglider.

Dad, as always, was in the right place at the right time. In fact he'd been on the main road just above where I landed just at the time I landed. He had thought about taking the small road that I'd landed on but decided not to, not knowing at the time exactly where I was. We worked out in hindsight that this was probably lucky as if he was coming down that road as I was trying to land on it, it could have made a difficult landing, much, much more challenging!

Now though all I had to do was walk. In all my planning I had sincerely hoped I would not have to approach Zermatt on foot, and here I was, still 25km away from the turn point at the Matterhorn, with nothing to do but trudge along the road. I was grumpy about this, but the sky was completely overcast here and out of all the people in the chasing pack who had taken different routes to get to here, I was the first one into the valley.

The walk was long, but at least navigation was easy – the main road took a pretty direct line up the valley, so no need for detailed map reading or tricky short cuts – just follow the tarmac. My good mood was somewhat dulled when I saw two X-Alps paragliders above me on the west faces 5 kilometres, or about an hour, further on. This turned out to be Ferdy and

Jouni Makkinon, who'd come across from the region of the Simplon pass, and were somehow managing to fly further up the valley than I had. But they too found the Zermatt valley devoid of thermals and landed about an hour or so in front of me. Out of all the people competing for third place (Maurer and Coconea were well in front of us at this point) there were the three of us slogging up the Zermatt valley heading south towards the Matterhorn, and then there were three others. Guschlbauer, Muller and Gebert who had all taken the brave choice to cross the Monte Rosa glacier this morning at 3500m. As I already mentioned, I thought this was a risky choice, because there was a high chance that it would not have been possible to fly down leaving them a long and difficult descent from the high mountains. As it was, the weather was kind to them and they were all able to launch and fly to the turn point at the Matterhorn at different times during the day. Whilst I was walking up the valley, Guschlbauer and Muller came through. Amazingly, given complete cloud cover and the now well established lack of thermals, the genius of Muller showed as he flew all the way out from the turn point to the main valley near to Visp. Guschlbauer meanwhile did something equally amazing – he took the turn point in the air and then turned south landing high up on the mountain in order to walk over on to the south faces, once again in Italy, and take the more direct, but bold, route to Chamonix. No one had ever tried this before and the rookie with only 6 years of paragliding experience was demonstrating he could play this game rather well. A radio journalist called me and asked me if I would be 'taking the Guschlbauer route?' Given I was still about 3 hours from the Matterhorn turn point on foot and would only get there about 6pm, walking over the main alpine chain at that point would be hopeless, at least Paul had the best part of the day still to fly it in (not that flying the area with a complete overcast sky had looked like a viable choice anyway, but somehow he had made it work).

So as I trudged up the valley, fellow competitors kept

popping out into the valley ahead of me. It didn't do great things for my confidence, but on the other hand, we'd all taken radically different routes to get here over the last two days (mine being the most circuitous) and still we'd all arrived within a few hours of each other.

I met up with Dad in Tasch. There are no cars allows in Zermatt so he had to leave the van here and bring the mountain bike loaded with drinks and food for the trip up to the Matterhorn turn point. I set off ahead of him while he sorted everything out, but quickly realised that this top bit of road was a nightmare to walk on so I switched to a path on the other side of the river and railway. This turned out be better for me, but no good for bikes so we ended up making our own way up to Zermatt. At one point Dad cycled up a track that he thought would join my path, but the footpath I was on actually went along the avalanche protection above the mountain railway. His path was down at railway level so the best we could do was shout to each other and agree to meet in Zermatt itself.

To the north of Zermatt there is a narrow constriction in the valley and just at this point is Zermatt heliport. Officially the heliport has a 2.5km radius restricted area or airspace around it, but locally it is accepted that as long as the paragliders stay to the south of the heliport, then there is no issue (in fact the landing fields are inside the 2.5km zone). For some reason this airspace was not on the list of airspace that the competition would control. The helicopters themselves approach the heliport from the north and it is pretty active, with plenty of wealthy people choosing helicopter transfers up to their luxury chalets. I was therefore shocked to see, as I came level with the heliport, Ferdy come gliding across pushing against the strong valley wind, with little ground speed, only about 100m above the deck of the Heliport! Brave, I thought! I was hoping firstly that no helicopter would arrive at that point, and secondly that he did not get arrested the minute his feet touched the ground! Being arrested would surely not be a good strategic move for his standing in the race!

I'd met up with Dad in the town; he'd arrived to see a procession of goats taking place through the centre of Zermatt. By the time we were walking through there together though there were only the droppings remaining. It was nice to be walking together for once. To get to the turn point there were two options: either continue straight ahead up a hill facing the valley wind, where I'd need to get to about 2000m to touch the imaginary cylinder that is the control point, or follow the valley round to the west where I could touch the same cylinder slightly lower, but with less chance to then fly back down. As I was pondering these choices I saw Jouni fly over us skirting along the west faces. It suddenly felt like a close race again, after days of being on my own we were all close together. Despite Jouni demonstrating both options were flyable I elected to continue straight up the into wind slope. It was a tougher and longer ascent but I hoped there would still be a chance of late afternoon thermals or restitution to allow me to fly down the valley. It was optimistic given the complete cloud cover and evidence to the contrary but I wanted to give myself every opportunity possible. As I made the final push up the steep hill I saw Micheal Gebert glide across and take the turn point in the air before turning back north over the town of Zermatt. In some ways this was good timing despite the disappointing information it brought: he showed me that the faces on the west side where he'd just come from were not really working. With no sun, he confirmed the only place where the air was going up was the into-wind face I was walking up.

My instrument played its little tune to say another turn point had been reached, and I looked at the slope above me for a spot to launch. It was horribly steep, the sort of slope where you need to make sure all your gear is tied to something to stop it rolling away down the hill, but I wasn't going to go any further. Airborne again, I soared in the dynamic lift, taking a couple of hundred meters in altitude. That was all I could do, it was rather nice being the air, but ridge soaring here would not get me anywhere and between Ferdy, Jouni and Micheal I'd seen every part of the slopes around Zermatt flown by some of the best pilots around, and I knew nothing was working, all I had in front of me was an into wind glide out towards the town.

Just as Ferdy had done before me, I found myself approaching the Heliport without a lot of height. There was a helicopter on the deck. Just before reaching the heliport itself there was a recognised paraglider landing spot, complete with a windsock. I had two options, push over the heliport as Ferdy had, and risk my safety and getting arrested, or land in the official landing spot with the wind sock, which happened to be right on the footpath I needed to be on. Crossing the heliport would have gained me very little against the wind in this narrow gap, and only created risk I was not prepared to take on, so I spiralled off my height and landed next to the path. When every meter in altitude had been so hard fought that day, it seemed strange to be having to spiral off height, but it was for the best. Desperate not to let my choice count against me, I packed quickly and resigned myself to repeating the long walk I'd spent all afternoon doing, but now in the opposite direction. With the exception of Guschlbauer who'd taken the brave route to the south, all of us in this group were now pitched against each other somewhere along this valley.

Arriving back in Tasch, the photographer Olivier jumped out in front of me and started snapping photos. It seemed he'd been assigned to Micheal Gebert, but Micheal was at that point siting on a low wall at the side of the road with blood pouring out of his nose. I was concerned for Micheal, but his supporter, Florian, was with him and they clearly had the minor medical emergency completely under control. So I just continued on down the valley.

Trudging back out of the Zermatt valley.
Photo: Olivier Laugero/Red Bull Content Pool

It seemed that the extreme effort of crossing the Monte Rosa glacier had taken its toll on the athletes that had gone that way. As well as Gebert, who I presume was affected by the huge changes in altitude he'd put his body through, Muller also told me that the push over the glacier was tough. After the race Muller explained to me that on that incredible flight out of the Zermatt valley he'd been so exhausted that he'd fallen asleep in his harness several times, and by Visp he had to land for his own safety. My route round via the north, had by comparison been quite easy going, I felt fit and strong despite all the walking I still had to do.

Although I walked throughout the evening on my own, Micheal and I ended up stopping for the night in the same layby, just short of St Niklaus. Ferdy and Jouni were a little bit further down the valley. So we now had a 4 horse race on for 5th place, and to see if we could reel in Paul or Martin in front of us. Maurer was now only 88km from Monaco and out of the reach of anyone else, Toma was just crossing into the Chamonix valley in second place. Our group of 4 had broken away from the rest though, with everyone else still to take the challenging Matterhorn turn point. Only 20 out of the original 30 teams were still in the race and spread out all the way back to the Piz Palu turn point. Being close to other competitors had awoken my competitive spirit and I was feeling pretty driven. I set the alarm for 3.30am with my goal for the next day being Chamonix and France.

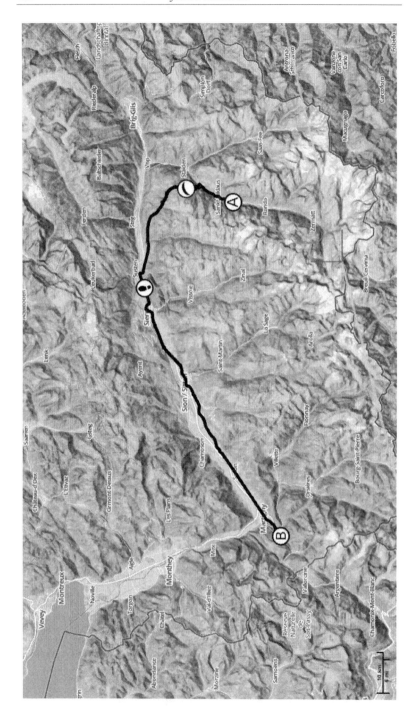

Day 11: St Niklaus to Le Cergneux

It was an early start day. This meant leaving the van at 4am. I've never been the best morning person, and as ever I was slightly behind schedule. As I pulled together my last things 4am ticked by and I heard the unmistakable footsteps of Michael walking past. Unmistakable, because no one else in their right mind would be walking along a main road in the middle of the Alps at 4am! I slid the door open and jumped out in a burst of energy that wasn't reflected in how I actually felt, 'hang on' I called as I set off only 10m or so behind, 'I'll walk with you'.

I wasn't sure if Michael really wanted my company or not, but from my point of view it was nice to have someone to talk to. If he felt anything like me he would not have planned for it but as it had worked out like this, it was a rather nice change from the tedium of walking on our own.

So we trudged on down the Zermatt valley, heading north and actually getting further away from the next turn point of the race – Mont Blanc. It quickly became clear that we both had the same plan, more or less. We'd walk down this valley until a convenient place to walk up the east faces and then we'd fly down into the Rhone valley, effectively cutting the corner we'd have to walk if we continued to follow the valley. This all sounds good but it quickly became apparent that neither of us really knew how to do this.

Toma Coconea had walked out of this valley a day
before but his route had started from much lower down, where
this valley joined the Saas valley. We wanted to avoid losing all
our height by dropping down to that point before ascending.
However the east walls of this valley were vertiginous and
looked more or less unscalable.

It doesn't sound like a major challenge – trying to find a
footpath out of the Zermatt valley – but it was. Between
Michael, Florian, my Dad and myself this challenge kept us
fully occupied for the next hour. Michal and I had maps,
Florian and my Dad had the advantages of being able to drive
around and had internet access with all the mapping options
that brings, but still it really was not obvious. The paths above
the village of St Niklaus itself looked less than ideal, so we
carried on walking down the road, all the time losing height.
From time to time Dad or Florian would pull alongside us and
drive at walking pace for a while as they relayed what they'd
discovered ahead. In some ways the campervans were like a
couple of giant Jack Russell dogs, running on ahead looking at
options and then scuttling back only to stay at 'heel' for a
hundred meters or so before charging off again. All this was
possible on a main road because, of course, it was not yet 5am
so we had the place to ourselves.

As light started to dawn Michael announced that he'd
take the Toma route. I was still sure there was a better way, but
between Dad and myself we couldn't quite find the way to get
onto it from the map. The path we needed to get to was a
switchback footpath up to the unpronounceable village of
Embd, but the road we were on was high on the East side of
the valley. We'd need to drop down to the bottom of the valley
and hike up the other side. According to the map there was a
footpath that took us straight down to where we needed to be,
but we were unable to locate it, so we ended up just hiking
along the road, leaving us the need to switchback down into the
bottom of the valley which would be frustratingly inefficient.

By this time Michael had also, independently, decided that this was the right choice and so we were still on a shared mission. The trouble was we still could not make any sense at all of where the footpath and roads were. I wasn't getting frustrated or annoyed: such emotions were not useful in times like this. Nevertheless, I simply could not get my head round it. We were all good navigators and yet we could not figure out something that should have been relatively simple. The map showed that a footpath cut down the side of the valley next to a cable car station. In this case I am not talking about a cable car station as in major ski resort cable car station. This was a single wire strung right across the valley supporting a tiny metal cage that could have held at best a couple of people. It also looked to be out of use. The light was better now as dawn was stretching its muscles, and I could see the tiny building of the other 'station' perched on the cliff on the other side of the valley quite a bit above us. The thin wire was barely visible as it approached the other end. This all had nothing to do with finding the footpath but it seemed important. Then I realised. This was close to where I'd landed yesterday. This wire was only about 500m further up the valley than where I turned to make my final approach to the little road and the bridge landing. A rather belated 'oh my god' feeling welled up in my stomach. A little bit more altitude yesterday and I'd have flown straight under, into or over this wire. And there is no way I'd have seen it from the air. I could barely see it from the ground and I was looking straight along it and could see both end stations. The brilliant Vincent Sprüngli had had to leave the race some days earlier after hitting cables in the Merano valley. His incident and what I saw today made me realise how vulnerable we are to cables. Normally when we fly paragliders we don't spend a lot of time low – rather our cross country flights are done following the high peaks, not scudding along low in valleys.

We continued past the cable car station, but I sort of knew what to do and where to go now. I say 'sort of' because it was not all fully clear in my head, but I suddenly had the conviction of someone who knew where they were going even if I could not explain it. The conviction was because I'd landed here yesterday, so I was now retracing my steps down the single track road I'd landed on to the very bottom of the valley.

I'm not sure, in hindsight, exactly when it finally became clear to us that much of the difficulty in finding the path was because this road was new. It was not on our maps. The railway had been re-routed here too. It was not a big difference but it meant it crossed the river at a very different point which was a feature I'd been trying to use as a reference in locating the elusive path. So between the road not being on the map and the railway being in a different place than expected it was no surprise that we were struggling to navigate. We may also have been a little bit tired and groggy given it was day 11!

As Michael and I reached the bottom of the valley both Florian and Dad were parked up nose to tail like some kind of reception committee. I only needed to swap some things around like leaving my head torch and taking my sunglasses, picking up a new drinks bladder full of sports drink and plenty of energy bars. My stop was a short one. Michael, on the other hand, was obviously going to need a little longer to sort things out - he said to me that he'd just be a few minutes while they got ready for the big ascent that was in front of us. It was clear they'd be doing this together with Florian taking food, drink and spare clothes for Michael. This was in contrast to my plan as I was now ready to set off up alone.

It is interesting here to reflect a second on the different tactics of the different teams. I know of many teams where the stated primary task of the supporter was to walk with the athlete as much as possible in order to reduce their pack weight to the absolute minimum gear that had to be carried. Indeed the few times I'd met with other competitors this was their approach. My Dad and I had taken a different tack. To us a kilogram of extra weight (which was typically more or less what was at stake) really made very little difference to the speed I could get up a mountain. On the other hand, by having my supporter on the ground in the van it meant he could always be with me very quickly as soon as I was on the ground. I've mentioned a few times in this book when he wasn't there in time, but these are notable simply because they were the exceptions. By contrast those that had their supporter hiking every ascent would often need to continue for hours on the ground before they regained contact, particularly after a simple fly down. For us our model was preferable simply because I felt it was the best way to keep me in good shape, well fed and in good spirits. The supporter's job is, if anything, harder than the athletes as they get less sleep and need to think of everything. Add a lot of hiking to that and something surely has to give. Anyhow, what is right for one team is not right for the next – I'm sure we were all happy with our own balance!

So, I was ready and Michael and Florian clearly weren't. I'd rather liked having someone to walk with but at the same time I was not going sit around and wait for them. In any case I was beginning to suffer from 11 days of walking and assumed they'd be quicker than me up the mountain. So I let them know I was going on ahead but that I'd see them soon when they caught me up. I really did mean it.

I never saw them. According to Dad watching on live tracking, as well as the head start I was going much faster. Something I had not expected. The path was incredible. It literally switched back up a cliff. From the bottom of the valley it was invisible, but as I climbed it revealed itself turn by turn, never giving away were it truly led. There was no chance of losing it though; there was no other way up this face! The slope eased from a cliff to merely breathtakingly steep and a few rambling building appeared. I had popped out at the bottom of Embd which seemed to be rather precariously balanced on the side of this cliff. It was all rather spectacular, particularly lit up in the beautiful morning sunshine with not a soul about given

the still rather unsociable hour of the day. Frustratingly I went
the wrong way, which, given my pride in my navigation and the
unbelievable mental hardship of retracing my steps was rather
annoying. Embd has a rather nice church, and the footpath
skirts around the church before arriving in what can rather
loosely be called the village centre. The road here was so steep
that the pavement was stepped. It was about this time I realised
I had a great deal of difficulty in putting my heel down on the
ground. It wasn't so much that it was very painful but more
that I simply didn't seem to be able to or want to do it. A
conversation with a friend a few weeks earlier came to mind
where he said he'd damaged his Achilles tendons by walking up
a mountain without putting his heels down. Because of this, I
made myself put my heel to the ground with each step despite
the fact that it was uncomfortable to do so. Then I realised I
had it back to front. It was because my Achilles tendons were
sore that I had the problem, not that it would become a
problem. Strangely, given how serious this could and would,
become, I didn't really waste much energy thinking about it. I
guess I realised that there was nothing much I could do but
keep on walking up this hill.

What a glorious hill it was! After the village came
woodland and waterfalls, sunny vistas across the valley. The day
was waking up and birds were singing. It was as though the
higher I walked the more life there was. The dark early morning
hours trudging along the main road in the valley were a million
years behind me. This walk is what the race is about – seeing
the Alps as no one, repeat no one, else sees them. Yes, you can
walk the same path, but the path is part of the whole journey,
the whole experience and everything I'd passed through to get
here seemed to be adding to and building on this very moment.
Up higher until finally I came through the last building high,
high up (over 2000m). It seemed to be a shepherd's hut which
stood on the tree line. Above me was only open mountainside.
As I clambered over the last stile I realised that despite being
still very much in the Zermatt valley, I could probably launch

from above here and fly around and out, saving me more walking.

But I needed to be higher. I left the path and headed straight up. It was ambitious. Straight up seemed to be rather more 'up' than it had looked from first glance, the grassy hillside belying the reality of the slope. The slope was so steep that I had to fold my poles away and put them in my pack as I needed to use my hands clinging on to tufts of grass to pull myself up. The hill was far too steep to launch from, but by now there were puffs of cumulus on these east faces. The paraglider pilot instinct in me started to get excited. The clouds weren't much above me now and I was still heading up desperately looking for a launch site. It was probably only 10mins or so before I found one, but it felt like an eternity. It was a small flat area just big enough that if I laid the wing at the back I could forward launch off the face.

It was only 8.30am but I didn't give it a second thought. In my head all I needed to do was glide to the north, round the corner and down into the valley. Although I believed this, I couldn't be sure of it because, despite the fact I'd walked up here with a reasonable map, it finished about 100m to the north of where I was now standing. No issue for walking, which after all was the main purpose to have the map, but it meant I had no idea what the terrain was like on the route I was about to fly. Not that any of this bothered me at the time.

Launching was straightforward and soon I was flying north hugging the slope. At the corner where the hillside turned back west there was lifting air. Despite it being so early in the morning, I didn't make the same mistake I had in the Dolomites. Instead I circled hopefully in the weak bubble of rising air. I didn't gain any height, but I didn't lose any either, so this lift gave me the opportunity to take time to look at the terrain round the corner, towards the west and plan my next step. What I saw was not really what I wanted to see. Indeed the mountainside did drop away to my west, but in front, to the north, was a great lump of hillside. To go around this lump would add a lot of distance – it was not a good option. But to go behind it meant passing over a col to my west. It just so happened that this col, still 2km away, was at the same height as I was at. That was not good news as I would not be able to glide over it from here.

By now there was quite a bit of early morning scraggy cumulus cloud above these north east faces, indicating more rising air. The terrain leading towards the col comprised of relatively shallow and predominantly tree covered slopes. Amongst the trees there were enough clearings to put the glider down in if I had to land there though. So, armed with this knowledge, in I went. About half way to the col I found a weak climb, enough to get another 30-50m. I was managing to stay at about the same level as the col in front of me. I was hoping to fly over it, however unlikely it still seemed. A little further along and I bumbled into another climb, same thing again. I was still only just making it back up to be level with the col at the top of each weak climb, so I needed every metre of altitude I could get. I had about half a kilometre to go now and it was still touch and go. I was hoping for buoyant air, if I could just keep my altitude at this height I'd scrape over. But no, it wasn't going to be. I started to sink and immediately I was looking for the best clearing to put the glider down in – the slopes were extremely shallow here and I was only just above them. It felt like game over.

A little further towards the col and the air felt better again. I began to hope once more that somehow I'd make it. But although I was in lifting air, I wasn't going up. I was flying as conservatively as it is possible to fly a paraglider and it was not enough, I was going to end up landing before the col. Just then, like some kind of divine intervention I saw a huge bird of prey next to me. He was off to my right further away from the slope. His wings were spread wide in the morning sunshine and he looked magnificent. No matter how often I fly with big birds of prey I never cease to be in awe of them. They know what they are doing. I was only just skimming tree tops, but without a thought for clearings to land in I followed him out from the hill. Sure enough, he turned, majestically, as if he was coaching me, leading me. He was my teacher, my trusted expert and he was right. My instruments confirmed it: I was once again going up. Two turns later and my friend was gone, but he'd given me the best present of all, the keys to a whole new valley system! I needed more height but I was going up nicely and after a few more turns the climb petered out and I pointed at the col with a new found confidence, I knew I now had enough height to clear the col. I was about to say goodbye to the Zermatt valley and say hello to the mighty Rhone valley.

I'd been so focussed on getting over it I hadn't really thought about the other side. After all, the ground dropped away nearly a 1000m to the valley floor and that beautiful vista was laid out before me. However it turned out that the col itself was deceptively shallow. After clearing the top, I then found myself on a touch and go glide skimming trees for the next 200m or so, before finally I could breathe easily as the tree covered slopes dropped away from me.

The wooded slopes I was now flying along were still NE facing (although rather more N now than E) and the cloud was clinging to the slopes above me. This was early morning cloud, cumulus, but of the type that pilots wouldn't normally look twice at. But I knew it was worth trying to stay up here. Despite the weak climbs, if I could manage to bimble along this NE face then I'd make considerably more progress down this valley than planned. It was only afterwards that the reality of thermalling on NE faces at 9am really struck home. This was an experience you just don't get through normal flying. This is why this X-Alps race is so special. The remarkable thing is my plan worked! Connecting with the first spine, I climbed 100m in about as many circles. I hopped along to the next spine, same thing. Way hey!

It couldn't last of course. The hillside curved away from the main valley as a side valley joined and all of a sudden I was unable to stay close to the slopes that were so generously keeping me up. Instead I was now gliding west along the south side of the Rhone and losing height fast. I'd completely bypassed Visp, by crossing the col, ahead of me now were Leuk and Sierre. I was trying to cling to the hillside, but as I lost height a plateau jutted out from the mountainside and power lines crawled round the corner on this step in the slope. I could squeeze through on the slope side, but I risked being stuck between the mountain and the power lines, depending on what was round the corner, so I decided to play it safe and cross the lines and move out into the valley.

The last part of the flight was fairly unremarkable. I was gliding down the valley and the only thing I needed to be careful with was that I did not go into the restricted airspace around Sion. My flight took me under the airspace as it steps down as it approaches the airfield. I was essentially flying along under a virtual staircase that I needed to ensure I stayed below. My flying instruments only show the position of the airspace and not the height that it starts and finishes at. The altitude the airspace starts at was obviously critical for me to ensure I stayed underneath it! Therefore the height information was provided to me on a piece of paper which was conveniently stashed between my hip and the harness, where I'd lodged it after take-off, for easy reference. Sometimes the simplest solutions are the best!

My glide was going to take me more or less to the town of Leuk. The last part was comfortable, smooth flying in morning air, with a surprisingly good glide ratio of over 20:1 at times, driven by the tail wind. It seemed that the wind in the valley was still katabatic here. Ahead of me though was a stretch of the valley floor covered in about 2km of forest. As I reached the edge of the forest I realised I was unlikely to make it across. The next landable field was still some way away on the other side. I started look round for options, I still had some height and I didn't want to squander it and land on this side of the forest. As I looked to my left for the first time in quite a while, I saw an X-Alps wing just above and behind me. It took me by surprise as I thought I'd been on my own for this flight. I assumed, wrongly, that it was Michael Gebert. The annoying thing was he had the height to cross the forest whilst I was pretty sure I didn't. I looked to my right and saw a football pitch near the road and on the edge of the forest. Reluctantly, I decided this was the smart choice versus a marginal glide over the forest. As I turned something else caught my eye. It was small and black and gracefully flying circles. Heading straight for the bird I knew I was saved. For the second time in this amazing flight the birds had marked the crucial climbs I'd needed. There was some convergence here and this bird was marking the best part of the lift beautifully. Half a dozen circles later and I had enough height to get over the forest. The climb wasn't going higher than that but now I'd be able to land close to my fellow competitor.

It was an easy landing approach, big space, no obstructions and into a gentle head wind. Despite this, I was full of trepidation as I crossed the road and looked down at the ground from only a few meters above it. I could not work out why I was so scared. Scared, that was it! That was the feeling. I was actually frightened of landing. It was the strangest sensation, especially after over 20 years of flying. It was only when my feet finally touched the ground that I realised in my head what my heart had known. My feet were suffering from 11 days of walking. Any impact, even just putting one foot in front of the other, was painful, so of course landing on them, no matter however gently, was something to be scared of.

Packing up, I texted something about it being an amazing flight to Michael who I still assumed was the pilot just a field in front of me. I walked along the road only to find my friend already gone. I was on the main road now and the

Japanese cameraman was there to film me walking along the road, at least until I met up with the van so I could offload some equipment and take on some food. I ended up eating the food Dad had got for lunch despite the fact it wasn't even 10am! I also found out that the glider that had come past me was in fact the flying Dutchman, Ferdy, and not Michael. Suddenly I regretted sending that text – what I'd written probably sounded like gloating, whereas it had not meant to be at all.

Of the 4 of us that had been close, 3 of us had walked up more or less the same path. Ferdy was much earlier than me and had followed the path around the hillside after the shepherds hut and not struck out up the face. He'd finally launched just above the col in a safe spot with a guaranteed glide out but still managed to climb before the col (higher than me in fact). He must have seen me fly underneath him and cross the col from where he was on the ground at the time. Michael was after me but had climbed above my launch spot before he dared to launch. He ended up having to land and hike up higher still to glide over the col, and in the end landed about 6km behind where I'd put down sometime earlier. So Ferdy and I were close and Michael not so far behind us, but what of Jouni? He'd taken a very different choice, to walk out of the Zermatt valley and up the south facing slopes above Visp. A good choice on a cracking day, but with Sion airspace to circumnavigate and a difficult forecast this was ambitious. As the day developed this choice turned out to be an error which put him far enough behind me to not to be an immediate threat. So just the Dutchman (in front) and the German (behind) to deal with!

The walk down the Rhone valley was punctuated with spectators coming out to meet me and walk with me for a kilometre or so. This did a remarkable job of breaking up a long and tedious walk. As expected from the forecast, the day deteriorated through the morning. With the sky overdeveloping fast and Sion airspace above us there was really nothing to do but to walk. I think that throughout that whole day Ferdy and I were never more than a kilometre or two apart, but I never saw him. We were so close but in our own worlds. Even just to see him on the horizon would have spurred me on. I saw his team van numerous times but never him.

I could tell the race was taking its toll on my Dad by now. He was continuing to do an amazing job, but he seemed worried that he didn't have food for another meal at lunch time, around noon (recall I'd eaten the lunch already!) I suggested that, as we were in the relatively built up area of the Alps, that he just buy a take a way pizza in the next town and we'd have that. Frankly by this stage of the race I didn't care what I ate as long as it was food! And so, just short of Happy Land (which is an unimaginatively named theme park), I stopped and dug in to a huge pizza. Dad told me to eat whatever I wanted and he'd have what was left. As I wolfed down a piece of it I realised that there was only one tiny piece left after that. Oops, I'd almost eaten it all and left him nothing. Oh well.

The rest of the day was walking and it wasn't a very exciting walk to be honest. I managed to find a cycle path that followed the river Rhone which kept me off the road at least. The only problem with walking along a reasonably fast flowing river for hours on end is that you realise that a canoe or just a rubber inner tube would allow you to cover the same distance in less time with significantly less effort. Having studied the rules in depth I knew there was nothing prohibiting this, but it was also not in the spirit of the race, and in any case I had no means by which to use this free transportation option.

Patriotic support arrives.
Photo: Jon Chambers

On the outskirts of Sion I passed a stationary Heinekin lorry. The driver leaned out to ask me if I wanted a drink. For a moment I thought he was offering me a beer! He was, after all, dressed in a green Heinekin uniform, complete with cap, driving a green Heinekin lorry with metre and half high letters proclaiming 'Heinekin' on the side! He was a follower of the race and was in fact offering me a bottle of water, which I gladly accepted. There was something special about this simple conversation. Then it dawned on me: he was talking in French. I'd crossed the language divide between German speaking and French speaking Switzerland. The realisation of this simple fact filled me with happiness. To me it represented the start of the final section of the race – through the French speaking part of the Alps. It was a milestone and it made my confidence soar.

After this it was a rather strange walk, past all sorts of forgotten industrial buildings, channels bringing water down from the mountainside and pipes crossing the river. It was such an industrialised area, notable for the total contrast to every other bit or terrain on this amazing adventure. I passed Dad asleep in the van at the side of the road. Damn, he made me promise not to do that again... but I didn't need anything and he looked so peaceful...!

Over the last few days I'd started to notice that my body was not giving me much notice when I needed to go to the toilet. I have no idea why this was happening, but it was on this walk that it started to get ridiculous. I'd be walking along quite happily when I start to feel the need to pee. I'd take a look around, see what hedges or such like would be coming up, but before I could even complete that thought, I'd realise that no, I needed to pee right now! This meant I ended up relieving myself in quite inappropriate places. I was even honked at by a passing car on one occasion. Maybe this is side effect of drinking litres of sports drink every day. Whatever was the cause it was disconcerting, and depending on the location, quite alarming!

Although I'd started the day with the vague goal to make Chamonix, as the day had progressed, I'd revised that to be the Col de la Forclaz above Martigny. It was still ambitious but it also represented a breaking point, away from the flat trudge along the Rhone valley and back into the proper mountains – Chamonix and beyond. It was still a long way away though. Believe it or not that last 14km into Martigny was along a dead straight road. Almost 3hrs without so much as a bend in sight. And all the time the distinctive bowl of the Col de la Forclaz didn't seem to be getting much closer. This wasn't just my imagination, in fact dark clouds were amassing in front of me and the col in front gradually disappeared as I marched headlong into grim weather once again.

By the time I reached the town of Martigny darkness was more or less upon us. Interestingly, this was the first major town on the route that my direct path was about to take me through the very centre of. It was quiet with sleepy cafes and bars around the central square and not too many people about. Despite this I felt extremely self-conscious. Physically, I was a wreck, I was walking with heel lifts to try to alleviate the pain of my Achilles tendons, but this had now resulted in my second, and rather nasty, blister of the race. I was wet, bedraggled and clearly exhausted and not walking well despite sticks clattering along the pavement. As the normal people of the world looked up from their Italian meal at the window of a restaurant, or across the top of their beer, I must have looked pretty grim – something the cat had dragged in.

Needless to say I didn't stop in the centre, but pushed on through the town eager to get up the pass to my resting place for the night. There was only an hour to go and I needed to keep moving. Somehow my brain had cut out all rational thought about what was reasonable. I knew I couldn't reach the top of the pass tonight but I was desperate to get as close as possible.

Leaving Martigny turned out to be not quite as easy as we'd expected. At the west side of town is a big roundabout where the main road leaves to wind its way up the pass, and a second major road heads up the valley towards Verbier. Neither of these roads were any use - I needed to be on the small and direct local road the headed more or less straight up. Dad was at the roundabout waiting for me, and was quite excited by the fact there was, as he put it, a fan club waiting for me. The 'fan club' consisted of a few brave and committed souls. I was delighted and impressed that people would go to the trouble of standing in the cold and rain at 10pm in the evening just to see a pathetic figure struggle past them!

I finally worked out that the little road I wanted left the road I was on before I reached the roundabout and the waiting fan club. I relayed this information to Dad who told me my fan club would be disappointed. Personally I couldn't really see how that had any bearing on the decision but I guess he was just trying to keep me in good spirits. After only a hundred meters or so the road I was on forked three ways and it was not obvious which one to take. As I was staring at the map and pondering my options, a couple of guys, one with a young kid on his shoulders caught up with me. This was my fan club and they were pretty excited to see me. I'm rather embarrassed to admit that I probably wasn't very nice to them. I didn't know which road to take so I asked them if they knew which one it was. They looked at the junction, but visibly had no idea (or so it seemed to me), nevertheless they appeared to be about to offer an opinion. Before they could do so I rather abruptly told them that if they didn't know just to tell me that they didn't because if there was a chance that I ended up on the wrong path I wanted it to be my doing only. It was a fair point but probably said rather grumpily and not in the best of spirits! They took some picture and wished me well. I was very glad of the attention, and of their persistence. So if you are reading this then I'm sorry I was miserable at that point, but please know that your support did help me emotionally on what turned out to be one of the toughest hours of the race for me.

As I started up the steep slope of the Col de la Forclaz, my arms started to really hurt. At first I could not understand why I had such unbelievable pain in my arms of all places. Then it dawned on me. My legs were so shot now and my feet were in such pain that I was using my poles more than my legs – I was literally hauling myself up using my arms. It was in this sorry state that a car swung around the corner of the road in the darkness and the rain. As the headlights swung across me I must have looked like an accident victim. The car stopped and the lady driver asked if I was alright. I think I was still in denial despite the obvious evidence to the contrary, so I said I was fine. Still she wanted to give me a lift to wherever I needed to get to, she was more or less urging me to accept help. I explained in my best French that I was fine, I was in a race and I couldn't accept a lift even if I wanted to!

My instructions to Dad were to go on ahead as far as he thought I'd make tonight and find a spot on my route to stop the van for the night. Once he'd found somewhere he'd then drive back and let me know exactly where it was. He knows me well and knew I needed to stop sooner rather than later, but at the same time knew I'd complain if it wasn't far enough up the pass. He went ahead just as far as he thought was necessary for me not to complain that it was too close!

When I finally did stop, we went through the normal evening routine. Sort out gear, get rid of wet clothes, drink recovery drink and get ready to sleep. I'd pushed myself harder today than any other day. In fact I think I'd pushed myself harder than I had at any other point in my life. My Dad looked me in the eye and told me he was proud of me for what I'd done that day. It meant a huge amount to me. Our family is very close and I'm sure through my childhood and youth he'd said he was proud of me many times before but I honestly don't recall a single moment in my life where it meant so much to me, and gave me so much internal strength. And indeed it was strength I needed.

After about 15mins of eating, drinking and sorting, I just needed the toilet then I was ready to get into the bunk and sleep. I slid open the side door of the van and stepped out. I had the intention to walk round the back of the van and across the road to some trees, but as soon as I put the weight on my feet I knew I couldn't do it. I didn't have the pack on my back anymore but I physically could not walk. It was all I could do to shuffle about a meter or so along to the front of the van, using the van to hold onto. I dragged myself back into the van with a sort of desperation. I felt absolutely beaten. I wasn't ready to give up but at the same time if I could not walk then I could not go on. I tried to ignore the reality of the situation as I finally levered myself into my bunk and more or less passed out into a deep sleep, not knowing what tomorrow would bring or whether I would even be able to stay in the race.

Day 12: Le Cergneux to Arêches

The ground race between Ferdy, Michael and me that had lasted throughout yesterday looked set to continue. Ferdy had stopped less than a kilometre up the col from where I was and Michael had spent the night down in Martigny. Having pushed myself to the very limit last night, and frankly having no idea if I'd even be able to walk this morning, I'd decided for a later start – 5am alarm. As it turned out, Michael started characteristically early, at 4am, so we looked set to be even closer together today.

As I set out that morning I was genuinely amazed that I seemed to be fine. Of course my feet were still a mess, but the stiffness and inability to walk that I'd experienced last night now seemed to have past. My legs hurt, of course, but importantly they seemed to be working ok. Sleep is an amazing healer! Taking the direct path through the last few chalets I popped out on the main road at a hairpin. On the outside of the bend, parked in a big lay-by, was Ferdy's giant campervan (the Dutch don't do small it seems). Whether they heard my sticks click-clacking on the tarmac or whether they saw me from the window, I don't know, but the door swung open as I approached and Ferdy stuck his head out to say hello. I was initially surprised that he was still in the van and making an even later start than me. As I came closer I started to realise quite how rough he was looking. He looked more exhausted than me and had a screwed up piece of toilet roll stuck up one nostril, clearly to stem the flow from a nose bleed. We exchanged pleasantries, but as he was obviously not about to start walking and I'd only come about a kilometre, I just carried on up the col.

The weather was still poor, rain and low damp cloud hung all around on the hillsides. Despite this the forecast was looking marginally better and between that and seeing that Ferdy was potentially suffering more than, I found myself in a surprisingly good mood. I recorded a merry video diary thanking everyone for their support and for the first time in the race I started to think about the finish. Maurer would finish the race at some point later today as he was only 67km from the finish line. That meant that I had 3 more days racing. With an improving forecast this meant Monaco was possible – challenging for sure, but possible. I believed it in my heart and it spurred me on as I crested the Col de la Forclaz.

From here I needed to drop down to Trient and then back up and over the somewhat higher Col de la Balme, which marked both the border with France and my entry point into the Chamonix valley. The valley was 200m below me, but there seemed no point at all in unpacking the glider because I'd have to wait for a gap in the clouds to launch whereas I could just walk down in 15mins or so. Instead I set off on a footpath that seemed like the most direct route versus the road which swung back to the right before switching back underneath me. I quickly realised though that the path was not a good option because it contoured round instead of dropping down. I really needed to be down on the road below me where after a 100m or so I'd be able to drop down on to a very direct path to the valley bottom. Between the footpath and the road was a grassy field, extremely steep, that seemed to turn into someone's garden which had a convenient track running down to the road. I got soaking wet feet scrambling down the slope through the grass, before rather guiltily cutting through this persons garden. At least it was still so early nobody would be awake!

I didn't stop at the bottom. There were some climbers

getting their gear ready to set off, presumably up onto the Trient glacier, but I just walked past them – I wasn't feeling all that sociable.

The walk up to the Col de la Balme turned out to be rather more epic than I had expected. With 900m of ascent it was a reasonable push, but given my state I knew it would feel like a lot more. The first part was rather pleasant though, walking through beautiful forest. About half way up the rain started. I put on my rain coat, and ploughed on as the rain became heavier and heavier. As I came out of the trees the walk was now also in thick cloud. It was wet, cold and I couldn't see where I was going. When finally the refuge on the Col came into sight it was a relief, but the weather was still grim. At least there was no wind to speak of.

I sought refuge in the refuge. I guess that is why they call them that! It was warm, and I took off the wettest items of clothing and put on my one dry fleece from my bag. I hung the damp clothes on various chairs and treated myself to an expensive hot chocolate and some *madeleines* (small cakes). I'd been carrying a waterproof zip lock bag with a 20Euro and a 20CHF note in it but this was the first time since leaving Salzburg I'd actually had to pay for anything myself. There were two hikers who, like me, were peering out at the rain. They turned out to be Catalan, and spoke French about as well as I did. I tried to explain what I was doing but I'm not sure they really understood (maybe I did have the upper hand in French after all!). The old man who looked after the refuge was reassuring them that although the chairlift was not turning at the moment, it was actually open. He proceeded to radio the operator to confirm and tell them there were 3 walkers here wanting a ride down. I tried to explain once again that there was no need, I had a quicker way down, but I still don't think I was able to explain it properly.

Finally, after 20mins, the rain eased and I walked across to the slopes to the north of the refuge to take off. The slope was steep and I'd gone some 10m or so above the path but as I began to lay out the wing the wind started to blow gently down the slope. I have no problem launching with a tailwind – there is no great magic to it – you just need to run very fast. With this slope it would be fine, so before the tailwind could strengthen I forward launched the wing, and was soon hurtling down the grassy slope as fast as my legs would carry me. What I had not really considered was below the path was a single wire fence, strung across the slope. I was fully committed now but it didn't look like I'd get off the ground before the fence. I became sort of fixated on it as I accelerated towards it. At the last moment I lifted my feet to jump it, but just at this same moment, as if by magic the wing took my weight and I was gliding away from the slope. It was a surreal flight out and down into Chamonix valley. I fly here a lot but I'd never been airborne on a damp day like this. The interesting thing was that the rain had left damp scraggy clouds hanging around the valley on this grey and drizzly day. These clouds showed that the air was rising gently there – not enough to climb of course, but by playing a kind of aerial join the dots I was able to extend my glide. At first I thought I'd make Argentiere, but as I sailed over the top the cable car station, and then the camp site, I realised I'd be able to glide half way to Chamonix itself. In fact I was beginning to worry about the exclusion zone around Mont Blanc which stretched down into the valley bottom. I could land before the valley stepped down at a little hamlet of Le Lavancher, or I could try to glide over the 'step' in the valley to an area that was built up and risk touching the restricted airspace. I took the safe option and landed at the end of the very last field I could find.

I'd been unlucky at the col because I'd arrived in grim weather and had to wait quite some time before being able to launch. Ferdy and Michael however, arrived minutes after I'd launched in the short period of flyable weather and had simply got their gliders straight out and taken off. Despite having put in a good start this morning they were now only just behind me.

Many pilots came to meet me as I walked down through Chamonix which took my mind off the walking at least. I passed Florian in a layby preparing some food for Michael who clearly wasn't far behind me. The weather was not really improving. Short sunny intervals would give way to masses of towering clouds and the occasional rain shower. Those low damp clouds still clung persistently to the hillsides. Somewhere between Chamonix and Les Houches a local pilot walked with me for a while and asked me what my plan was. I explained I would walk up to the Prarion and fly from there down towards Contamines. He looked up at the east face of the Prarion, now directly ahead of us and surrounded by cloud and told me that it wouldn't be flyable there today. Perhaps tomorrow, he said! I patiently explained that I would fly from there and rather arrogantly pointed out that I fully expected to be in Beaufort before the day was out.

Glaciers peeping out from the cloud in Chamonix valley.
Photo: Jon Chambers

I met up with my family in Les Houches who'd driven the short distance from Geneva to come and say hello. I think I looked a bit of a mess as my youngest daughter looked at me with the kind of look that says 'what on earth are you doing' and then refused to come near me!

After some lunch I set off up the mountain, whilst my Mum, wife Ali and my two daughters took the cable car to the top. We'd agreed to meet up at the top and they carried some spare water and warm clothes for me. As I met up with them, the wind picked up and the sky looked black. It looked stormy and foreboding. I started to think that flying wasn't such a good idea after all. But it was a difficult call because if I wasn't going to fly I could walk straight down the other side, but if I was going to fly I still had another hundred or so meters of ascent and a kilometre or so to walk across the top of this hill. The decision seemed impossible and I threw my poles to the floor in a fit of despair, but I hadn't really got the energy to be properly annoyed. My mum took my two daughters back to the cable car, whilst my long suffering wife, realising I needed moral support, stayed with me. I decided I needed to at least try to fly, so I set off, wife in tow, for the take-off.

Remarkably, the take-off was fine, clear of cloud and the wind was lighter than the gusty, stormy period 20 minutes before on the other side had indicated it would be. There was a guy standing at the launch waiting for me, Michael and Ferdy to arrive. Another avid X-Alps fan, waiting on a mountainside for a few mad athletes to struggle past!

Whilst conditions at launch were fine, towards Les Contamines it looked black and horrid and it was clearly raining. I decided things were quite likely to get worse rather than better and so elected to launch anyway, on a certain glide into the rain. With a goodbye kiss to my wife, and an easier take off this time around, I was once again airborne. My trick of following the scraggy clouds worked once again, as I crossed from one side of the valley to the other to follow the best looking parts. Although I never actually went up by doing this I was managing a glide of about 30:1 at one point! I finally landed, under sustained rain, just short of the point where a path and the ski lifts head up towards the Col du Joly – the fourth col of the day for me.

I waited a couple of minutes for Dad to catch up in order to get some food and change some kit around. I was surprised to find my reading of the weather was wrong. I was right that it was changeable, but it was actually changing for the better, not the worse. As I sat having a cup of tea I found out from the live tracking that Michael and Ferdy were both airborne, and were now thermalling in the sunshine. If there is a higher being up there somewhere controlling the weather then it seemed that he did have a sense of humour, but I'd rather he hadn't chosen me as the butt of his jokes on this of all days. Talking to my wife later she'd passed both of my close competitors on her way back down from the launch, it was clear that we were still neck and neck even after 11 days of racing! Still, right at this moment they were busy thermalling on the other side of the valley while I was sitting drinking tea in the van. It was a sign that I needed to keep moving. With the sun shining, but changeable weather clearly the on the cards I set off with only light clothing and a thin rain jacket for the showers.

I never actually saw either of the other two in the air, but as I walked up the spine that my path followed on its way to the col, I could see Michael in a car park below me where he had landed, only a little further down the valley than me. Surprisingly Ferdy had landed about where I had too, so in the end my sneaky glide in the rain was more or less equal to the two thermals they took to get to the same place. I wasn't glad, but I was sure as hell relieved, if they'd flown over my head at that point I'd have been insufferable!

Col du Joly was another 900m ascent back up to 2000m. The first part was pleasant enough but then it started to rain. Soon the rain turned into rather more sustained rain and all of a sudden I found myself walking into thick cloud. There was a distinct sense of déjà vu! I glanced at the altitude on my watch; I was still more than 300m below the height of the Col.

This was not a good sign.

I was beginning to get cold and I was pretty soaked through by the time I did reach the col. I'd only brought the minimum clothes to wear on the walk up and the light jacket clearly was not up to the job of keeping me dry in this rain. Now that I was at the top, in cloud and pouring rain, I realised if I waited I'd get very cold indeed. Knowing that I was 300m up into the cloud convinced me that there really was not much hope of flying. What surprised me though was that there was a building here, right on top of the col, with a road up to it. I hadn't realised there was a road here, so I called Dad on the phone to see if he was close by and could bring me dry clothes. He was on his way but was still a long way off. I hadn't given it much thought but every col I'd walked up and over today he'd had to drive round. And most of the drives were not straight forward. This last one would have involved driving back north to St Gervais, up to Megève, over the mountain via the resort of Les Saisies and then down to and back up the Hautluce valley. If you don't know where those places are then trust me – it is a long drive! So rather depressingly I started walking slowly down the mountain, following the road. After only a 100m or so, I changed my mind and decided I be better off waiting for him, that way if the weather did improve and it stopped raining, and the cloud cleared then I might still be able to fly. But I was freezing by now. I stopped by a gate leading to field, sat on my wet rucksack, arms around my knees hugging myself and trying to stay warm. My Dad was trying to get to me as fast as he could but he was still a way off.

It was about at this point, that I noticed it had brightened up slightly. I looked behind me and was amazed that I could now see the col. I stood up and realised I could see the valley below me too. It was still raining persistently, but at least there was some visibility now. Just then Michael glided past me on the other side of the valley. Arrrgghhh, once again I had arrived at a col at just the wrong moment only for one of my competitors to arrive a little while later when the conditions were just right! For this to now have happened three times in one day was downright annoying. I clearly was not going to stand for this. Despite the rain, I didn't want to miss the potentially narrow window of opportunity, so I climbed the gate to the field in front of me and got my glider out. Back on day four when I'd been discussing flying in the rain with Thomas De Dorlodot, he'd given me a tip. He told me that when launching in the rain you should unfold the glider as the very last thing you do and launch immediately, so it doesn't get too wet and become difficult to launch. With no time to lose I threw the gear out and climbed into my harness. I realised I hadn't called Dad with the change of plan, but it was too late to do so now, the glider was already out in the rain, so with another concerted run I lifted off straight into the very wet air.

The road that came up to the col wound its way up the rather steep slopes below and to my right. Sure enough, as I glided out from the hill, there was our unmistakable Pringles van, climbing obediently up the mountain side. In it was my father, who luckily was driving a 'zig' rather than a 'zag' and so was facing the point at which I was flying from. I have no idea if at the time he swore, having just driven a whole valley that he needn't have driven. But by the time we did meet up he seemed to have come round to seeing the funny side of the whole event as he watched me merrily fly over his head in the opposite direction.

If lady luck was being rather nasty to me when it came to take off timing, she was making up for it with nice glide lines. Michael had flown down the east side of the valley, whereas I'd flown down the west, again sticking to those damp bits of hanging cloud. I didn't see where he had landed, but checking the tracks later I saw that I'd landed some 2.5km further down the valley than he had, and that was from a lower take off point. Still, it wasn't all down to the sneaky glide. I'd pushed it as far as I could – with the valley dropping at only slightly less than my glide angle those last few kilometres had seemed very close to the ground. I knew the valley dropped more steeply at the end as it joined the main valley with the town of Beaufort nestled below. The problem was I couldn't see round the corner. Finally the ground was catching up with me. A small road snaked its way along the left hand side, but below it there was a 50m deep tree lined gorge. It was tempting to continue which would mean dropping below the road, using the gorge to continue, but a slight bend meant I couldn't see what was ahead. Finally, at the last possible opportunity, I swung the glider in and landed on the little road where it wound round one of the spines before diving back into the trees. Looking at the map after the race, I'd have needed a 10:1 glide to make it out through that gorge and over Beaufort, and on average on that flight I'd only had 8:1 (not bad considering it was raining hard!) so it was definitely the right decision.

I started to pack up in the rain and as I was folding the glider I noticed a small tear along the trailing edge. I guessed it had probably been there since that jagged launch at the top of the Stelvio pass, but now I could see it I needed to fix it. As Dad got the repair kit from the van and we set about the task of repairing the glider in the middle of a single track road in the rain, a local chap came by to talk to us. It turned out that he was a hang glider pilot and he couldn't quite believe I'd flown today. Once again I have to admit that the conversation was a little half-hearted from my side as trying to repair the glider was taking most of my concentration.

Dad went off ahead to Beaufort to prepare some food. After a couple of kilometres of walking the rain stopped and the road emerged from the gorge. Incidentally, the gorge had a cable strung across it at road height, so even if I could have out-glided it I'd have been cheese-wired trying it! With a clear view of the valley I once again considered launching. The wind was blowing down the hill though and the height difference to Beaufort below me was only a couple of hundred meters so it made sense to walk. I found a footpath that cut down through a verdant grassy field. The trouble was it was pretty slippery with the recent rain leaving the grass soaked, so it was difficult to go quickly. All of a sudden my feet went from under me and I heard an almighty bang. I'd landed on the ground with a bump in a seated position. No harm done to me, in fact the ground was rather soft, but in the process of falling all my weight had gone onto my right pole which had snapped in the middle. The race was not only taking its toll on me but also on my gear. These poles were fantastic, super light and foldable so easy to fit in my harness but now I'd need to manage without them.

Finally I got to Beaufort and the enormous supper that was waiting for me. I wasn't done for the day, not yet, but there was some work to do. As we had all expected, Maurer had crossed the finish line earlier this afternoon, so now I knew that I had less than 48hrs to try to finish this race. Less than 48hrs to do 230km. It was only going to be possible with making the absolute most of the flying. I had one advantage though on my competitors: this was my back yard. This is where I fly day in, day out. I know my way around here, and know where to get the right forecasts from and, just as importantly, I knew who to call. The forecast for tomorrow was for good thermals starting surprisingly early in the morning. That was the good news. The bad news was that the cloud base would only be 1700m in the morning, increasing to maybe 2000m if we were lucky. That doesn't bode well when there are 2500m mountains to cross on course. After wolfing down my food I called my good friend and local ace pilot Damien De Baenst. We had a chat about the options and what was possible. I think Dad was beginning to get annoyed with me talking for so long when I should have been walking, but this was important, and I needed the maps and forecast in front of me. Damien was a great help, but what I really needed was someone just to make the decision for me. I wanted Damien just to say 'go there tomorrow' but he understandably wouldn't – it was a big decision and I needed to make it.

After much deliberating I decided I needed to launch from above Montgirod. That meant quite a lot of walking between now and 10am tomorrow when I needed to be taking off. It had been such a tough decision I almost called Michael and Ferdy to confer with them, rather like Thomas and I had shared information back in St Moritz. However the competitive nature got the better of me. We'd been in a close race for the last two days and if there was a chance for one of us to break away it was for sure tomorrow.

So finally, I set of walking towards Arêches. It was already after 10pm and Dad was starting to get worried about the 11pm compulsory stop. As I climbed out of the town, head torch on, following the footpath that cut straight up the hillside, Dad set off to find somewhere for the night. He announced there were two options, a layby where Michael and Florian were set up for the night or the village square in Arêches itself – there was nothing else in between. It was about 10:15pm as I passed a footpath sign saying it was 50mins to Arêches. That was it, I would make it to the village easily. A few moments later my mind was made up for sure as I passed the layby where the Germans were parked. They had passed me during my prolonged dinner stop in Beaufort.

It was raining again as I approached the quiet and sleepy village of Arêches. I'd had a good day today but I needed to rest now and I was mentally beginning to power down as the lights of the village came into view. Yet there seemed to be some slightly odd lights at the edge of the village. Next thing I knew a great big white dog came bounding towards me. He was the advance party, come to greet me and welcome me to this village high in the Beaufortin. The lights appeared to grow umbrellas, and then they became people standing underneath them. Finally, as I walked the last few meters they started to applaud me. I felt overwhelmed. I was so tired and so surprised by this reception committee that I didn't know what to do or say. Honestly I can't remember what I did say. But for so many people to come out on a wet evening and stand in the pouring rain at nearly 11pm at night was remarkable. So people of Arêches, I am eternally grateful for your welcome. It lifted my spirits. It made me proud to be me. Nevertheless this race didn't allow us much luxury in enjoying these moments – I was aware I needed to make it to the van in the village centre before the cut off. My new friends told me where to find it.

As I arrived at the van, a car pulled up with some of the people who had generously welcomed me into the village. They offered me a hot shower. Their house was 100m away. I would have loved a hot shower, but having mentally arrived at my resting place for the night my brain could not cope with walking one meter further. Somehow reading my mind, our hosts offered to drive me in their car. There is nothing wrong with this, as far as the rules go as long as you restart each morning from where you stopped you can do what you like in the rest period. But nevertheless it somehow felt wrong. It felt bizarrely like it would be cheating. I was also acutely aware I'd need to be up at 4am if my plan to get out of here was going to work, and I needed my sleep. So rather reluctantly I declined the kind offer. In hindsight I rather think the people of Arêches may have thought me quite rude, I barely stopped when they came out to greet me and then turned down their generosity when they offered me a shower. But I certainly did not mean to be rude, so let me say it now: thank you people of Arêches!

Once again we had stopped in the centre of a village, unusual in a campervan, but something you can get away with if you only arrive at 11pm and you are leaving again at 4am. The advantage of this was that there was a public toilet next to the van. A real toilet! What luxury.

But despite the welcome and the amenities there was bad news in the van. It was extremely serious; in fact, it risked putting a stop to our whole race. Every night my Dad had, with great glee, joked about making up my 'night time bottle'. This was in fact a protein recovery drink from High 5 made up with milk and powder. Still, my Dad liked to point out that even though I was 36 years old he was still drying my toes (and if he was feeling very childish, singing 'this little piggy went to market...') and making me a night time bottle, just as if I was I was a baby. Anyway, up until now the recovery drink had been chocolate flavour and so each night I had a bottle of chocolate milk to drink before bed. Tonight he broke the bad news to me, there was no way to put it gently so he just came right out and told me. We'd run out of chocolate milk. It was a disaster. I had to drink pink milk instead!

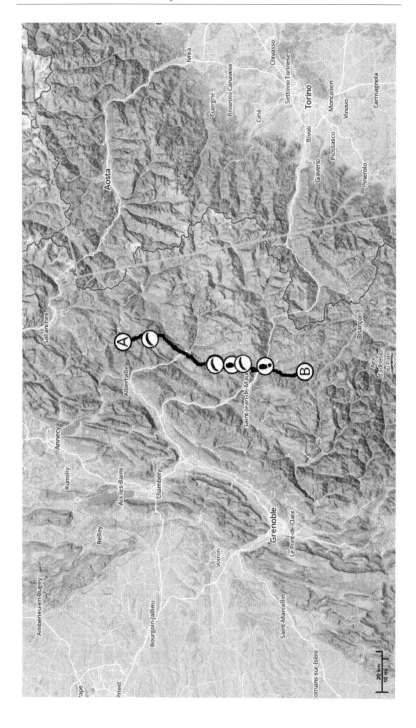

Day 13: Arêches to somewhere on the D902

I had to make it over the Col de Galibier today. Famous for its regular inclusion in the itinerary of the Tour de France bike race, it separates the northern and southern French Alps. As such it marks the point at which the weather changes. It really is as clear cut as that. Whilst in the north we'd have a moist air mass with a low cloud base today, the south would have great thermals to over 3000m. It was simply different air down there. I needed to find a way to get over the col and cover a reasonable distance on the other side. If I didn't get over the Galibier then there would be no way I'd be able to arrive in Monaco before the cut off at 4.22pm tomorrow.

With this in mind I started early on the long and arduous trudge heading south, up past the Lac de Saint Guérin and up to the ridge line high above Aime, in the Moutiers valley. The walk was pleasant enough, despite being extremely muddy underfoot. The lake itself was stunningly beautiful. The morning was in contrast to the previous days, with a clear blue sky and still air. It was the sort of morning and the sort of walk that makes you glad to be alive. Even after 13 days of this race I found I could enjoy the walking, enjoy the scenery, simply enjoy being on this journey.

Still, I knew this would be a tough one, so Dad had once again taken the van as high as the rough track would allow and then set off on foot with me, carrying a rucksack with food, flying clothes, maps and plenty of drink, whilst I carried just the minimum equipment. Even by 8am there was cumulus forming on the eastern slopes. The cloud was very low though, as we climbed up it was already below us. I was nervous about today, I needed to fly a long way but I couldn't really see how it would be possible.

The walk up was not actually very steep, instead the path climbed gently through undulating mountain slopes, all the time taking us in the direction we needed to go, as well as higher. Soon we were walking through cloud and it was difficult to work out where we were. I knew on the map the point I needed to launch from, but it was hard to know if we were there or not. Finally, we found ourselves contouring along a grassy hillside. It seemed to face the right direction and we seemed to be more or less at the right altitude. We were clear of cloud but everything in front and below us was full of cloud. Even though I knew it would be a straight glide out over the valley there was no way I could launch here and stay within the rules. So I sat and waited, and ate some food. After about 10mins the cloud started to clear and, almost imperceptibly slowly, what looked like a lake came into view. Odd, there was no lake on the map. We stared harder into the murky cloud and the outline started to become better defined as the cloud thinned further. Suddenly it came into focus – it wasn't a lake, in fact it wasn't even horizontal – it was a patch of snow belligerently clinging to the north face just across from where we sat. This was even more odd because there was not supposed to be a ridge of a mountain there, right in front of us, it was supposed to drop away down to the main valley at Aime. As the cloud cleared further the shape of the mountain to our west came into view and suddenly it all became clear. We had not walked far enough, we needed to go another kilometre or so along this path until we came out on the correct slope, which did indeed face out into the main valley. We grabbed our things and walked quickly along to the right spot. I had the feeling the time was right to launch and so I had switched from being relaxed and waiting to now being impatient to get to the right place. It was still early but the clouds were bubbling up from these south east faces, if I waited too long the cloud might close in completely, filling in the gaps and not let me fly out from this point, high up on the mountain, at 2400m.

As I'd broken my trusty folding poles yesterday I'd walked up here with standard telescopic walking poles that we had carried in the van as spares, and for my Dad to use. The problem was that these did not fit in the pocket in my harness. I considered putting them in the back pocket but leaving the ends sticking out, but I wasn't happy. The problem with this is that there is a danger that lines can get caught around the poles either during launch or if I suffered any incidents in flight such as big collapses. Dad weighed in with the fact he didn't think it was such a good idea either, so rather reluctantly I left him with the poles as I got ready to launch. It turned out to be the right decision, given the epic events that I'd have to overcome later that day. The take-off was nice and grassy but it was downwind again. The slope in front of me was quite shallow, but I expected to out-glide it, so, with a good clearing in the cloud in front of me and my Dad poised with the video camera, I charged off the hill.

Paragliding is an amazing sport. We get to travel along and see parts of the mountains most people will never get to see. We get to see herds of Chamois and Ibex, fly with great birds of prey and enjoy some stunning vistas. But even for an experienced alpine pilot, flying amongst great towering clouds is a special experience. We don't often get to go higher than the cloud base so it simply is something we don't experience very often. But when we do, like I did on this morning, the experience is magical. It is like you are flying through some kind of fairy tale, at any moment you might chance upon a giants castle up here, or a magical beanstalk! My long, long glide took me round the edges of some mighty clouds, great masses of fluffy cotton wool with ethereal wisps all around. I skimmed round the sides and brushed against their misty tentacles. I was in another reality and it was incredible. And why, oh why, did I leave the video camera with Dad to just record the take off!

My nirvana amongst the clouds continued as I came out into the main valley. Turning to the south west to follow the edge of the valley, still I was above the cloud base. I started to look at my altimeter with concern. I'd dropped below 2000m and still there was no sign of the bottom of these clouds coming into view. I was to the side of the clouds out over the main valley but I needed to get under the clouds so that I could then use the thermals to stay more or less at the base of the clouds as I continued my flight.

When I did finally get to the cloud base it was around 1700m. This is very, very low. But, on the positive side, just as the weather forecast had predicted the thermals were already good at 10am. The question was simply where could I get to with such a ridiculously low base? I was in no rush as I knew as the day progressed the cloud base would get higher. Now that I was in the air I needed to fly very conservatively, to stay airborne or at least to stay high. Once below the clouds I found that the strongest climbs could be found on the valley side of the cloud, where wisps formed below the cloud base. I initially expected these to turn into thick cloud lower than the main mass of cloud, but in actual fact these areas of strong lift seemed to be taking me at least 100m higher than the cloud base before the white stuff engulfed me and I needed to move out into the valley again. After some time working these to see how far I could climb up the side of the cloud in this way, I came to the conclusion it was not very far! All the time I'd been working my way along the valley and I was now level with the Montgirod launch, a place I've started distance flights from before. This time, however, the cloud was only just above the take-off. I considered top landing here, waiting for the conditions to improve and then continuing in an hour or so, but, thinking back to the thermal forecast for the day, the cloud base was not expected to get that much higher. So I carried on.

Next thing that happened was that I ran out of mountain and cloud. Despite the low altitude I had been working with up until now, I had been cruising. That is, I was flying along with guaranteed climbs, marked by the unbroken cloud along this south east facing ridge. I was now approaching Moutiers and I needed to cross the valley here. This was such a short transition (about 5km) that I'm not sure I'd even blink on a normal cross country flight, but from this altitude it was going to be touch and go. There were no clouds on the other side and I'd arrive below the tree line, meaning no chance to land high either. I set off but after only about half a kilometre I chickened out and flew back to the last cloud, finding the strongest part right on the edge and squeezing every meter I could from the climb without going into the cloud. This was as good as it was going to get.

I arrived on the shallow tree covered slope with only 1200m. There were no clouds above me but there were clouds further on. Fortunately, the thermal gods were smiling on me today and I found myself in a gentle but beautifully smooth climb that took me high enough to connect to the better climbs further along the ridge. I was back to cruising, staying close to the terrain in climbs reliably marked by small scraggy clouds. I was still on the east faces and heading south. But, I was heading south into a dead end. I wasn't concerned at this though, as it was part of the grand plan. By now I was approaching St Martin de Belleville, on the route up to the popular ski resorts of Les Menuires and Val Thorens. I could see the towering buildings of Les Menuires in the distance. My planned route wasn't going that way. There was a fork in the valley here - I was going to fly down the westerly valley – an uninhabited valley with no road. The reason for this bold choice was because at the south end of this valley the Col was only 2300m, much lower than the 3000m plus terrain around Val Thorens.

I had to glide across another valley entrance to get to the last spur before the valley I needed to take branched off from the main valley. Once again high voltage power lines ran up the hillside here and I found myself thermalling dangerously close to them to get back up to a reasonable height. But as low as the clouds were today I couldn't get back up to them. I hopped across to the next corner where the mountain turned to face more southerly, but this turned out to be an error as the valley wind was blowing now and the wind on the corner was breaking everything up. There was cloud above the hill I was on, but it didn't seem to be forming from here, it felt like it was forming off the bowl to the south side. I could maintain altitude soaring this face, but if I got too close to the corner my speed increased and the lift was gone. I considered my situation and realised that if I went around the corner at this low height I would not get back up, so I needed to get more height here. I told myself to be patient. I told myself I needed to be back up to 1700m before leaving here. Backwards and forwards I went. Nothing was working. I tried to climb out on every little bubble, until finally there was one that felt a little stronger so I went with it, turning circles as the drift of the wind took me round the corner, past the point of no return. It was nothing. I'd just done what I'd told myself not to do. I'd gone round the corner and now I was facing a glide to nothing.

The power lines I'd been climbing over a little while earlier snaked over the top of the lump of mountain I'd just flown around, and now they dropped down through the middle of a bowl I was flying into. Some hikers waved from a path that followed around the back of this bowl. It was pretty, despite the electrical cables, as the bowl was carpeted in high mountain meadowland. The slope in front of me looked like I would be able to soar up it in the valley wind. At least I would have been able to if there weren't sodding great big power lines at exactly the point that I'd need to be scratching along the grassy slope. Damn and blast. Below the lines the slope was very shallow and there was nothing to do but turn and land more or less under the lines.

I packed quickly and hiked up under the cables. I walked straight up 200m vertically. I was well above the power lines but the breeze I'd been hoping to soar in was very, very light. I re-launched and then spent the next 10-15 minutes zig-zagging backwards and forwards at the same height. I got to know every gorse bush on that slope very well indeed. Finally I found a good climb on the spur and I was able to claw my way back up to cloud base. That should have been it, I should have been on my way again, but instead I made a dumb decision. I was on the south face, but as the valley swung back to running due south this side of the valley once again became the east faces. I stayed on this side. What I should have done here was to cross on to the shallower, but sunnier, west faces. I don't think I'd appreciated how much time had passed given how slowly I'd had to fly and the intervening hike to get past the power lines. In my head it was still early and the east faces would be working just as well, but in reality the sun had swung round and the clouds above the east faces turned out to be just wisps blown over the ridge from clouds forming on the other side. In hindsight I think exhaustion was probably affecting my decision making here. I realised my mistake, but by the time I did it was too late. There was some lift on the east face and it prolonged my inevitable landing in the valley bottom. Inevitable because the ground was rising fast, and despite a higher cloud base deep in the mountains here (up to 2000m now, whoopidy-do!) it was still impossible to fly through the Col whilst staying clear of cloud. Besides, whichever side of the valley I'd taken I was approaching a clagged in col from the north side. I was always going to have to walk over this one, I'd just hoped for less walking.

Despite the dumb decision, I still landed at 1800m with only a 4km walk to the col. I smiled to myself as I realised this was higher than the cloud base was back at 10am in the Moutiers valley. The first part of the walk was easy as it was along a track. However the track only provided access to the power line pylons and I left it to take a more direct route for the last couple of kilometres. Walking on the track had been fine, but once I left it every metre became much harder. I tried to follow a vague path but it was nothing more than a sheep track and it soon petered out. What had looked like easy going grassy terrain from afar turned out to be rough and tufty and interspersed with patches of 2 m high gorse bushes that needed to be traversed. Without poles and after 13 days of this, it felt extremely hard. It became worse for the last part as the ground rose sharply, without poles I struggled to keep my footing and I feared losing my balance at any moment.

When I made it to the top it was notable only for the fact it was entirely uneventful. I felt almost let down. Having walked up the north side, I'd been entirely clear of cloud, but here on the ridge was a great wall of cloud glued firmly to the south side. Because of this there was no impression of the ground dropping away (although it did, quite dramatically in fact), nor was there any view. It was all highly unsatisfactory for the climax of what had felt like an epic ascent. Of course in reality it was a minor 500 metre height gain over a few kilometres, but it felt like a whole lot more. To the left of where I'd reached the ridge the power lines that seemed so intent on staying friends with me today, disappeared into the great wall of cloud with that characteristic humming they make when surrounded by water vapour. I walked along the ridge peering as well as I could into the cloud, trying to find a way down. This morning I'd flown down to cloud base but this time I'd have to walk down to cloud base.

The descent took me to a boulder strewn flat area surrounded by an amphitheatre of rocky slopes. I was still in cloud but every now and then I got glimpses of something below me. Something looked like a line, maybe a track. It was difficult to tell. I stopped, because this was a launchable spot if the cloud would clear. I was obviously on the edge of the cloud and it was clearly a very deep cloud. Everything in front was in shade so this part of the cloud wasn't likely to be too active – as long as I could get off the mountain here in clear air I was certain I'd be able to stay below it. But it was a big 'if'. I wasn't even sure what I was looking at in front of me. From the map I knew I was at the back of a huge bowl on the north side of the Maurienne valley. But what was it below me? Just like earlier this morning when the snow field had looked like a lake, there was no depth to the vision. Gradually what looked like a flat expanse of ground came into view with a track running across it. Indeed the line was a track. But it looked very flat and very close, perhaps only a 100m below me. I shook my head as though trying to make the cloudiness clear from my vision, but of course it had no effect. I was right on the edge of the cloud band now it was clear enough to be able to launch but I was worrying about not getting away from this place. The power lines buzzed menacingly from somewhere hidden inside the cloud off to my right and I was beginning to think there was little chance that this would work. Then, just like the lake had turned into a snow field, the vision became clear and this time my reading was right except for one important point. The ground I was looking at was in fact a long, long way below me.

Satisfied, I walked a little further down (to be sure to give some leeway to the cloud). This made the launch more 'interesting', from a nasty rock strewn gorge, but quite feasible. It wasn't long before I was back in the air and cruising south, close to the cloud. The other side of the valley was the Col du Galibier, and I was now feeling more confident. Cloud base was higher and all I needed to do was cross this valley and get up on the other side. I didn't need to fly over the Galibier, I just needed to get close enough to cross on foot and fly again on the other side. I was feeling confident, I had a plan, I was in the air and there was still plenty of time left to fly a long way. Little did I know then that life was about to get a whole lot more difficult. The scariest moment of the race was still to come.

Crossing the valley was not entirely straight forward.

The Maurienne valley is deep and narrow and the valley winds howl through here, feeding the multitude of thermals that are generated in the great mountains towards Italy in the east. The col I'd launched from was set back a long way from the valley, and gliding out from it I could see the road past Valloire and up to the Col du Galibier on the opposite side of the valley. The valley wind was coming from my right, and if I followed this bowl round to my left I'd end up too far down the valley to make it back against the valley wind to where I needed to be to cross the col. That left the right hand side of the bowl as the only option. There would be a good climb on the spine at the end, but to get to it I'd have to fly round the leeside of the spine. Even at close to 2000m the valley wind was clearly evident. Pushing round the spine was really unpleasant. It was extremely rough in the lee due to the turbulence from the rotor and the sink was dire, but I knew I just needed to squeak over and I'd be on the windward side and into a certain climb. What I did not expect was that the tree covered mountain slope that I was flying around was actually a vertical cliff on the other side. As I pushed over the edge my heart was in my stomach as the ground dropped vertically away. I'd just pushed over a knife edge spine into a strong wind!

The expected climb was there but surprisingly slow, but once up to cloud base (now at 2200m, things were looking up!) I was ready for the crossing. I pointed the glider at the Col du Telegraph rather smug that everything seemed to be going to plan. The glide was rather buoyant and I expected to arrive over the top of the fort that guarded the col du Telegraph.

The Col du Telegraph is a rather odd place. I don't consider it a col at all, because in actual fact the road only goes over a finger of rock that sticks out into the Maurienne valley. The road does drop on both sides, so I guess in that respect it is a true col, but when you see it from the air it feels more like a crest on a road contouring around the mountain. What you don't see from the road is the mighty fort that still belongs to the French army. It is an obvious place for a fort with such a commanding view of the narrow gap in the valley. It feels like in ancient times they probably didn't even need weapons, you could more or less through stones down on your enemies from here!

The fort itself was at 1600m, and I figured if the worst came to the worst and nothing was working I could land just behind the fort on the access track or near the road. I knew it would be rough here, it was in the lee of a bigger lump of mountain that stuck out into the valley, and at this lower height the valley wind was clearly already strong. I was within a few hundred metres of the fort when the glide turned from being rather good to being utterly terrible. I was in strong sink. After just a minute in this sinking air it was abundantly clear I would no longer be arriving above the fort and all ideas of landing up here were wishful thinking. I ploughed on hoping things would be better closer in. In fact it got worse. I was being thrown around the sky and furthermore I seemed to be barely going forwards despite the fact I should have been flying downwind. I always fly with a kind of mental map of what the air is doing around me, adjusting it as I experience different things that I don't expect. This time though I'd just torn up my mental map and hurled the pieces into my imaginary waste paper bin. I suddenly hadn't a clue what was going on, and it was truly scary. As I was being thrown around, I glimpsed a tiny puff of cloud form directly above. At that point my instruments told me I was going up. Salvation, I thought and gratefully threw the glider onto its wing tip and dared to glance at my vario – I was going up pretty fast. I was, however, more or less sideways because I'd thrown myself into the turn so aggressively. This was mainly to keep the energy in the wing and to try to avoid collapses because the air really was horrible here.

Banked over and climbing and with a tiny puff of cumulus above me I thought I'd get out of here. It was a fleeting thought, and entirely premature. Feeling like I'd hooked the thermal, I started to let the circle widen, not a lot, but enough to go from wing over in lift to a proper thermalling turn. What happened next, well, frankly I don't know. I must have had a complete blow out because of the severe turbulence. I was being thrown around like a ragdoll, I glanced above me to try to see what the wing was doing. Was it flying? Was it collapsed? Was it tangled? I couldn't answer any of these questions as I couldn't see the damn thing! It was definitely behind me though so I hauled on both brakes and as I fell below it and it came back into my field of view, I released gently. The glider came straight out, flying properly. At that point the thought that flashed through my head was thank god I'm flying this wing. Despite having just flown it into about the worst air imaginable and taken an almighty hit in the turbulence, it came straight out when I needed it to. Nevertheless the self-congratulations on having the perfect wing for this adventure were only momentary as of course I was still in exactly the same predicament. I glanced up and that little puff of cloud was gone. It was almost as though it had only appeared in order to put its thumb on its nose, waggle its fingers and taunt me! At least I hadn't had my walking poles sticking out of the harness to tangle with the lines during that blow out. That really would have ruined my day.

My only thought now was for my own safety. The race was forgotten as I pointed towards the main valley to get out of this god-forsaken place. It had, after all, just nearly killed me. I was now pointed straight into wind and really not going forwards very much. I squeezed the accelerator bar and thankfully edged out of this gorge, now far below the fort.

I was still 700m above the valley floor and the wind down there would be nasty so I looked for somewhere to land on the mountain side, where the road wound up to the Col du Telegraph. There was nothing, not even a stretch of road without trees on the downhill side. The wind was already blowing hard at this height, the trees were heeled over and thrashing about and it would be even worse lower down. I looked around desperately but I could not see any good options. I lined up directly over a small field surrounded with trees but even 300m above it I couldn't keep the glider centred over it. I needed somewhere bigger in these conditions. Much bigger. My time was running out. I was fine flying here but connecting with the ground was inevitable, it was just a matter of time before I ran out of altitude. However I managed to get back onto the ground it was not going to be pretty. I felt like I was suffocating, there seemed to be no options as I supressed a rising panic.

The bottom of the valley was very built up, and where there weren't trees there were wires criss-crossing the bottom. The only option was a large service area next to the motorway that dominated the bottom of the valley. There was a big area of tarmac for lorries to park on and thankfully there were no lorries on it. I aimed for the middle of it. It sounds easy. It wasn't. There were several problems. Firstly, from about 200m above it I was not going forwards, unless I had the accelerator bar pushed but this makes the wing harder to fly. I dared not go near the back of the area of tarmac in case I got blown backwards into trees, buildings and assorted bits of motorway slip roads. The problem with staying in the middle though was that I was in the lee of some pretty tall trees. These would be creating severe turbulence to add to the already tumultuous air that I was desperately trying to keep my glider above my head in.

This was it then, I had played my cards and made my choice. I just needed to hold on and hope I managed to get away with this one without any broken bones. It was going quite well until the last 30m. I think I must have hit the rotor behind the trees, because my wing took a massive collapse, I didn't have time to look at it but I could feel exactly what had happened, I must have lost most of the wing from the left side, because now I was in a hard turn to my left, facing the ground and accelerating fast. All I could see was a single story toilet block with a car parked outside it with a canoe on the top. It was as though I was in free fall – I was heading towards it at a colossal speed and at that point I was sure I was going to hit it. All this happened in a split second, and in that same split second, without thinking about it my piloting instinct had kicked in. All my weight was hard over to the right in the harness and I had as much right brake on as I dared, trying to straighten out the wing. Nevertheless the car and the yellow canoe now filled my vision. Just when it seemed to be too late, I straightened up. Now only metres off the ground the ordeal wasn't over yet.

There was a small patch of grass in this service area for picnics, and it just so happened that a young family, a couple with a very young daughter, were having their lunch there. They'd spread their rug out between the trees and the small building, obviously trying to find a little bit of shelter from the strong wind. They'd probably seen me above them as they ate their lunch. I imagine first with passing interest, and then perhaps with a bit of trepidation as they'd seen me getting thrown around and finally alarm as it seemed certain I was going to crash.

At this point I was entirely oblivious to the presence of the young family. Miraculously I'd managed to level out the wing, but I was now about to hit a small bush on the edge of the picnic area. I crashed through the upper branches only to see a small girl of about 3 years old who'd run across to see me. Oh my god, no, I thought – she was right in my path and I was out of control. I don't know if her parents called her back or the basic human survival instinct in her took over, but just in time she turned and ran back toward her parents. And so I landed. Smack in the middle of the grassy picnic area.

Everything switched into slow motion. Lots of things started happening, but it was as though I was watching it all on a TV screen. I was somehow separated from all this carnage around me. Two policemen arrived on the scene. The family, who had been enjoying their picnic now had one wing tip from my glider thrashing about menacingly on top of them. The other wing tip was hooked up in a small tree. Another car turned up. The policemen were talking to the family who were now hurriedly packing up their things. I stood there still in my harness, in some kind of trance, all these things going on around me.

The policemen came over to talk to me. Here we go, I thought. I've landed on *autoroute* property and nearly maimed a small child. This clearly was not going to go down well with the French police. The funny thing was I didn't care. I was alive and unharmed which was, frankly, quite amazing. By comparison, anything else that could happen to me now would be insignificant. The first word the policeman said to me was 'X-Alps?' Surprised, I managed a weak 'yes'. 'What can we do for you?' were his next words. It was probably then that I realised I was in shock. I was still in my harness unable to do anything useful and I couldn't even think what help I needed. My lack of response led him to take some leadership over the situation. 'How about a ladder to get the glider out of the tree?' he suggested, and immediately got on his little walkie-talkie radio and summoned the motorway maintenance van, who must have been only a matter a metres away because he was there in seconds! I was still extracting myself from the harness whilst the policemen were already busying themselves with untangling the wing tip from the tree. The other car that arrived turned out to be avid X-Alps fans that had been tracking me. Soon my Dad was there as well, having parked just outside the fenced area of the *autoroute* and climbed through a broken down gap in the fence.

As the shock started to edge away from me a sort of calm descended on me. It was 4pm. From all the way down here there was no way I could get up to the Col du Galibier in time to fly down the other side. I hadn't yet checked that on the map, but in my heart I already knew it. With that one mistake went my hopes of finishing this race on the raft at Monaco. The X-Alps fans turned out to be a very nice chap called Pierre-Louis and his girlfriend. They pointed out to me that my fellow competitor was above me and they pointed to a white glider just a bit further down the valley climbing away. What?!? My first thought it was Ferdy or Michael, man would I ever shake those guys off? But then Pierre clarified it was in fact Martin Muller. I felt both better and worse at the same time. Better because it meant I'd caught and momentarily overtaken Martin for 4th place, but worse because he was still up and flying whilst I was here on the ground and lucky to be alive. I knew Martin would still fly far and it made me frustrated for what could have been, what I'd just thrown away. So I watched as 4th place flew away from me, and packed up the wing.

Dad brought cans of Red Bull from the van to say thanks to everyone. I asked Pierre if he knew the most direct way up to Valloire. Indeed he did, but rather than just tell me he offered to walk up there with me. This was great! But before I did anything I needed to stop and eat. We crossed back to the van but found that the motorway maintenance guy had repaired the fence in the short time we'd been there, so we had to climb it!

The intensity of the race was taking its toll on our provisioning, but it didn't matter, we'd prepared for that. Dad boiled some water and turned some freeze dried mountain food in a bag into a surprisingly tasty Chicken Tikka Masala with rice for two people. Well, it said two people on the packet. Once again Dad never did actually get any. In between mouthfuls of food I was able to quickly calculate the distance and height gain needed to get up to the col, and indeed it was impossible to make it before 9pm. However, the other thing I learnt from checking the live tracking was that both Ferdy and Michael had made very different choices to me this morning and, as it happened, both their choices turned out to be very wrong.

They were still on the far side of the Madeleine, and frankly in no danger at all of getting close to me today. So with 4th place having disappeared out of site, the col not reachable and no one challenging me from behind I suddenly felt very relaxed about everything. The walk up through the forest with Pierre-Louis was pleasant enough and he did indeed know the most direct route, finally bringing me out onto the main road just before Valloire. At one point the west facing ski slopes above me looked promising in order to catch a few late afternoon thermals, but I felt like it was clutching at straws, the chances it would get me up were slim and walking on the main route up the Galibier seemed like the easy thing to do.

Just after Valloire, my wife, our two daughters and my mother caught up with me. Mum jumped out and agreed to keep me company as I walked up the road. I can't remember what we talked about but the company made a pleasant change to the monotony of trudging along a main road. The walk up from the bottom of the Maurienne valley had been a long one, and the day was drawing to a close. Dad was parked up ahead preparing supper, which, in his own words was only a light supper of omelette and mashed potatoes. My wife stared in disbelief at my plate which was piled so high it looked like a sculpture of the Matterhorn! Half of the plate was made up of a mountain of an omelette, filled with mushrooms, peppers and the like and the other half was made of the biggest heap of potatoes you could imagine. Dad and I had become used to how much I was having to eat so it seemed normal to us, but now with someone else to view the spectacle it was quite apparent it was not so normal! 'How many eggs are in that omelette' asked Ali, my wife. 'Oh, 8' replied Dad, nonchalantly! With the hearty supper inside me, I was ready for the next part. The female folk set off back to Valloire to find a hotel, whilst Dad went onwards to find a layby for the night. Meanwhile, I continued walking.

Anyone who has driven or cycled the Galibier will

know that it is in fact a very long way from Valloire to the col itself. The road gradually climbs up a long and bleak valley, devoid of anything but the most basic vegetation. After what seems like forever, the road turns and rises steeply, but just as you think this is the last push it opens out again in a huge curve around a plateau before finally making the last switching ascent for the summit. I knew all this was ahead of me – we'd driven here in spring time during training, when we had to dodge the numerous marmots who thought they still had the road to themselves on that early morning. It was with this memory in my head that I was rather taken aback to stumble (almost literally) upon a music festival taking place half way up the long push from Valloire. So surprised was I by this that I snapped a picture to send to the diary. A rather grumpy security guard then gruffly told me that photos were not allowed, which given I had taken it from outside the perimeter, seemed a bit extreme. Given he'd been grumpy about it, I told him in my politest French that I was deleting it, just as I pressed 'send' on my smartphone and sent it to my diary page on the X-Alps webpage. 'There', I thought to myself 'I've only posted it to a website being followed by 2 million people…' I guess I was just feeling rather rebellious at that point.

Meanwhile Martin was already near to Briançon, some 30km to my south.

The only thing left to decide, as we prepared the van for the night was the strategy for tomorrow. The weather would be similar to today, excellent flying conditions to the south of the Col de Galibier, but difficult for those still to the north. This made it rather easy for me as I was only an hour from the top now and could easily fly far in the good conditions to the south, whilst those behind me would most likely struggle. The problem was it was too easy. I'd tried flying the east slopes from Galibier before and they don't really work, but from midday the south west faces are perfect for flying far and fast. Even though I could start at 4am and I could launch from 5am, for the first time in my race there seemed to be no point. Whichever way I looked at it, pushing hard in the morning would only give me about a 10km glide down the valley for which I'd then have 2-3hrs trudging back up a hill to find a place to launch to start a proper distance flight from. That distance could be covered in about 20mins once conditions became good. The logical thing to do then was simply wait on the col until the sun came round and the thermals started to work. So given I only had an hour to walk up to the col, then logically I could have a rather luxurious lie-in! This simply didn't feel right. I could imagine myself waking up at 9am in the morning to one of my competitors walking past the van, somehow having made up a phenomenal distance. It was impossible, but a part of me simply couldn't accept not getting up and pushing on. Finally, over the pink milk (blurgh!) we came to compromise. We'd get up at 5am (already a generous lie-in by X-Alps standards) and I'd walk up to the col in first light. Once there we could assess the situation and where the guys behind me were and decide whether to glide down and push on or whether to wait for the thermals.

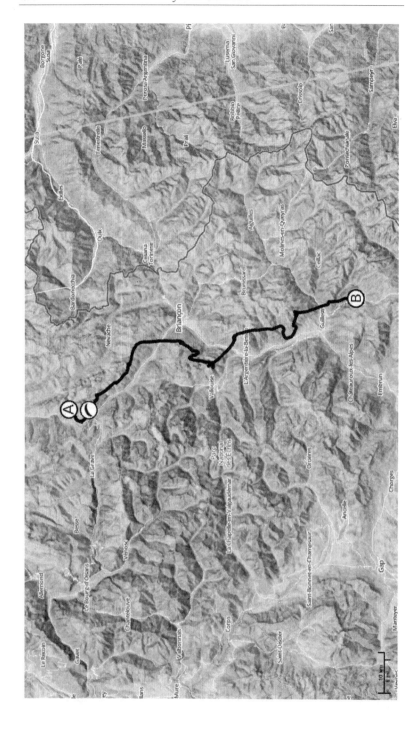

Day 14: Col de Galibier to Vars

My dawn walk up to the summit Galibier was magical and special, once again this time of the day felt like the best time as the mountains were deserted, the air was clear and cold and the place simply made me happy to be alive. As always I cut across country to take out the giant curving bend in the road but in the process found myself in a boulder strewn telly-tubby land, where the ground continuously dropped down and then up again in great sweeping curves. I began to wonder if this time I should have just stuck to the road. In one of the dips I noticed the high mountain flowers seemed to be slightly white. On closer inspection I realised there was a light frost, no wonder I had to keep moving to stay warm!

Just as I was cursing leaving the road, it swung back in front of me and I re-joined it for a while. The road climbs the last steep section in a serious of tight hairpins, but there is also a tunnel here to short cut the top section. Back in spring this final part was still closed due to snow so I'd actually launched from the deserted road at the top. Now it was summer everyone would be going to the summit, just because it was there. For me, of course, there was no choice, tunnels were against the rules.

I made the highest point about 7am. To my north a blanket of low claggy cloud indicated my predictions about the weather were quite accurate, whilst to the south the sky was clear. We checked our position against the others and confirmed, as expected, we were in absolutely no danger of being caught – they were still about 60km away without many flying options. And so we made what was probably the most difficult and frustrating decision of the race: we sat and waited.

We shot a short video for the diary. It was lucky we weren't in a rush because between Dad not being able to work the video camera and some early bird tourists making a lot of noise, it took us about 4 takes to record a simple video. Next some more breakfast, before we finally agreed I might as well catch an hour sleep or so. So paranoid were we that Dad promised to stay in front of the live tracking in order to make sure the situation did not change dramatically. So, against all my X-Alps instinct I climbed into my bunk in the middle of the morning and had a snooze.

I awoke to the voices of crowds of tourists. At first I struggled to work out where I was and what I was doing, but then a wave of panic came over me. I was in a race, what was I doing asleep! I sat up, all flustered and absolutely sure that I should be doing something other than this. When I finally did calm down I realised that, no it was alright, strange as it felt this was the game plan. Sit in the van and wait.

Constant checks outside the van were starting to worry me though. At 7am there had been a gentle breeze through the col from the north, but by mid-morning that had built up into a consistent wind blowing over and down the side I needed to launch on. It was now too strong to launch here. I was hoping that the sun would bring the breeze up the slope but somehow the way the valleys connected here made me think that there was a good chance that it wouldn't change.

We needed a contingency plan, and so over a cup of tea and packet of Jaffa cakes we decided we'd need to contour along the mountain side to the south and get away from the col which was clearly funnelling this north wind over. Mum, Ali and the girls came by once more and after a quick chat I decided it was time. This was the final play, the race finished at 4.22pm and with luck I'd be cruising at around 3000m at that point with the sea only a few hours flying further on. Dad came with me, as we tried to find somewhere to launch. Given there was no vegetation it should have been easy, but it wasn't. I expected to only need to walk a short distance from the Col, but finally we had to walk three kilometres until we found a slope where the breeze was only cross slope rather than downslope. It was now after midday and I was scared of getting this wrong. I was scared to launch and land at the bottom. After all this was a place I didn't know at all, and even though it all seemed like the right thing to do doubt kept creeping in.

The take-off should have been fine, but the slope was steep, and I pulled the wing up in a reverse launch in a stronger bit of wind, but this proved to be a mistake as I tripped on the turn. The slope was so steep that I only stopped tumbling down it about 20meters lower down. In the process I'd now ripped the nose of my lightweight pod harness. Minor war wounds, no big deal. Second time I was off without a problem and immediately turned south, along the bottom of the rocky crags.

Round the corner out of sight from my Dad, I linked into a very weak climb. It wasn't much but it was enough to tell me I would not end up at the valley floor, that I'd be fine now. I relaxed into the flight. My plan was to be conservative, to stay up and not to take risks. So with that in mind I made sure I was up to the top of the cliffs in this weak bubble of a thermal before I started exploring further, looking for something better.

I climbed up to the cloud base which was lower than I expected, before crossing over a valley in order to continue towards Briançon. I was feeling confident now, the mountains in front of me were clearly generating good thermals as there were good clouds and I was content just to link one to the next. Or at least that had been the plan. After the short crossing I was back down to the shallow lower slopes, and the valley floor was still quite high here so there wasn't a huge amount of height to play with. I felt confident I'd climb at the first spur, but there was nothing. Still nothing at the next one either, this was beginning to look bad. My ground speed was very high and clearly the north wind was still in evidence blowing down this valley and probably was responsible for the unwillingness of nature to provide thermals where there really should have been some! Crossing a gap over a flattish, dampish area of grassland and wondering where I'd manage to clear the next spur, the vario finally began to sing to rising air. Why on earth there was a thermal here I don't know, but I was in no position to be fussy! I worked it patiently back up to the clouds and now, finally, I was rewarded with flying straight in lifting air under a nice big cloud. Finally I was covering the kilometres. This is what I'd waited at the col all morning for. This was what would cement my fifth place in this mighty race.

The next section of the flight was one I'd done before in practice, but that was the only time I'd ever flown here before. As I was not so familiar with the area I probably didn't choose the best route. Near to Briançon I crossed the valley to the peaks behind the Serre Chevalier ski area. With nice clouds and rocky faces in the sun it looked easy. However, on arriving I found a clutch of people standing on the edge of the hillside flying model gliders in the best bit of lifting air. Initially I was unfazed, I was above them and flew straight to their spot expecting to climb out from there. It didn't happen and despite exploring the hillside for something that was going up, I ended up gradually loosing height until I was in danger of becoming entangled in someone's pride and joy of a model. Still I was still reasonably high so once again I pushed on. All the time the clouds had been growing quite big and angry to the north of me, not yet storms but it looked like it might go that way. Towards the south was better so I needed to keep moving. I was getting low and flying against a valley wind now, so again I had to take a weak climb at the next spur to get myself back up high, I worked hard in a windy gully to finally climb clear but as

I did so I started to hear a strange noise from above. It was a sort of pitter-patter noise coming from the wing. I looked up, rather slow on the uptake until finally it dawned on me. It was raining. The wretched cloud had the cheek to rain on me! It was only light but not a good sign. I needed to keep moving south away from the congested mass of cloud to my north.

The next lump of rock that I jumped across onto had huge towering cliffs facing into the bright sunshine, it was also facing the valley wind and had a nice cloud above it. This is about as close as you can get to the perfect invitation. The view down the valley towards Embrun was stunning now, and as I approached the peak in front of me I started to see it in more detail. Standing like the majestic spires of a cathedral, almost perfect towers of rock stood separate from the main cliffs. There were several and they must have been 300m high, shooting vertically up, almost like a needle. I was going to arrive just above the top of them and I could not resist flying over the main one and looking straight down it. As I did so I saw a lone climber quite near the top. He was a mere dot on this mighty tower of rock. I was in awe. This guy must have the same incredible view down this valley, the same amazing privilege to be on top of this slither of rock, but the difference was he had climbed it, all I'd had to do was turn in a few thermals to get here. What's more his presence made me realise the remoteness of the place. On a paraglider I'm only a short glide away from a nearby town, but for him getting down would not be quite as easy. Looking back to the north I shuddered – there was a storm building, although he probably couldn't see it yet. I wouldn't want to be where he was if it did break…

I'd expected to hit a strong thermal and leave this place behind in no time at all but I ended up once again scouring cliffs looking for a climb. When it came it was weak, and I never really got high. Finally, I decided time was getting on and I needed to keep moving, so I crossed the valley to the other side. I was going to arrive low and this time there was no cloud to mark where I should fly into and furthermore the valley wind would be strong on the face I was going to arrive at. Now given I'd just left a peak that should have been the perfect thermal trigger without much to show for it and was now gliding into an iffy one, I was quite surprised to find a good climb in the other side. Good, but not good enough as it turned out as the wind was breaking it up as it blew it apart. I pushed back into wind to the same trigger point, this time to be rewarded with a 6m/s climb all the way to 3500m. Wow. Now I felt invincible. At this altitude there was none of the southerly valley wind and south of me every peak and ridge was covered in sailplanes. I was expecting to cruise now, but unfortunately paragliding cross-country flying is somewhat of a roller coaster experience. I crossed the next couple of peaks high but without finding a repeat of the strong climb I'd just used to propel myself to this altitude. Ahead of me were indeed sailplanes dotting most of the ridges, but I started to realise they were flying backwards and forwards, rather than going round in circles. Where there are thermals gliding aircraft of all types go round in circles. They were also rather low compared to me. In fact, all of them were rather low. I started to realise that they were simply soaring the south faces in the now ferocious valley wind. As I dropped into the valley wind my progress became more and more difficult until finally I needed to cross to the next hillside, and found myself having to push the accelerator in order to creep round low onto the shallow slopes. Progress was painfully slow, and it was starting to get rough. I began to realise that instead of looking ahead along the slope I needed to look down it as there was a danger at this rate I wouldn't even out glide it. Finally, I was beaten, I wasn't going to make it round so I pointed out at the valley and tried to glide out of the nasty gully I'd ended up in. The glider danced around in the turbulence, but it was nothing compared to yesterday's ordeal. Finally I made it out of my gully and pushed along a low slope heading south. I was now literally only a few hundred meters from the valley floor and was back to picking great big fields to put the wing down in, backwards if I had to! It wasn't over yet though because the low slope that I was on happened to have the full force of the valley wind hitting it. As I crept along it with a ground speed in the low single digits, I was at least going up. I kept going in a straight line, and miraculously I kept going up. The valley turns here, and the valley wind was coming from the west before turning north. I was now soaring along the face that was scooping up the wind spilling through the gap at Embrun. Soon I was back to 2500m. Not as high as before, but out of the main effect of the wind and now able to jump into the entrance to the Col de Vars, the penultimate major col before the last push to Monaco.

But Monaco was impossible, time was almost up. I knew I'd done enough so I was relaxed. As I flew into the valley that leads up to the Col de Vars, I joined a weak climb. It was taking forever to gain height in this climb and a quick glance at my watch told me that it was almost 4pm. A sailplane came through my climb and rejected it, choosing instead to continue contouring along the hillside heading south. He didn't seem to be losing much height so I decided I'd push on. If I spent another 20mins in this painfully weak climb the race would finish in any case, so I might as well take one last roll of the dice. Sailplanes have significantly better glides than us, and I soon realised my assessment was wrong, there was no lift on this slope and I was soon gliding towards the ground. The bottom of the valley had power cables criss-crossing it and for once there was no need to press on. I was near a minor road leading to the village of Vars itself, so I turned into wind (coming from the north now in this valley!) and touched down in a nice little spot near the road.

That was it. It was only just after 4pm, but there was no need to pack up in a rush, there was no need to shoulder the pack and keep moving. I took a picture of the storm clouds to the north and posted the final entry to my diary, 'not quite over, but I've done enough to keep fifth place'.

I sat down next to my unpacked gear and thought back to those first moments at the start in Salzburg and what I'd been through since. The race had been an all-consuming experience. I thought about my desperation on the Dachstein. About the great leaps I'd made through the field on the third day and the nearly terminal mistakes I'd made in the Dolomites. They all seemed so long ago; already consigned to history. So much had happened in the race. I felt like I'd experienced every season and weather condition, from the scorching heat of the Gaisberg to the blizzard on the Bernina Pass, but the strongest memories of the weather were of wind and rain. Whilst I'd spent little time with any of my competitors during the race itself, an inextricable bond had been created between us all. We'd been here and done it and only we knew what it was really like - no one else could relate to our experiences.

When I started this race I was only an eager and well prepared rookie. Looking back at the first day of the race was like thinking back to my first day at school after just completing final exams – I realised now that I had known nothing then. The learning curve had been steep, but I'd climbed it. I'd climbed much more besides! I'd covered over 1500km to get here, little more than 100km short of the finish line. I'd covered just over half the distance in the air and the rest on the ground. I had raced over 60km and more than 3000m of ascent by foot on average every day for more than thirteen continuous days. The bizarre thing was I didn't feel tired mentally or physically. Three days earlier near to Martigny I had been exhausted, convinced that I'd be unable to keep going, but now I felt fine. I'd just completed the last day of the X-Alps and it was the easiest and most relaxing of the lot!

Through all of this there had been one person who had been my life line, who had kept me sane, kept me fed, kept me believing in myself. I owed every bit of success in this race to the amazing support I'd had from my father. Always where I needed him, never complaining, never questioning, just quietly getting on with what needed to be done, even in the most extreme situations.

Race over! Final landing spot in the Col de Vars.
Photo: Margaret Chambers

I was still lost in my thoughts when moments later my whole family turned up with a bottle of champagne. And so it was that I sat on a rather scrawny piece of grass, high up in the Col de Vars in southern France, surrounded by my family and drinking champagne. Finishing on the raft in Monaco would, of course, have been my first choice, but as that wasn't to be then somehow finishing like this seemed right, in peace, in the mountains surrounded by my family and drinking a rather fine bottle of bubbly. Cheers!

The end!
Photo: Felix Woelk/Red Bull Content Pool

Appendix 1: Equipment & Preparation for the X-Alps

Preparing for the X-Alps race required a lot of planning. The success of our team was, in no small part, a result of the huge amount of preparation that we put into the race. I've captured here our approach, what we did and how we went about getting ready for the race. I'm not saying it is the right way to do it, we probably could have improved on many things, but somehow, when we put it all together it worked for us.

Getting in

The first thing you need to do is actually get into the race. Probably an obvious statement, but it is really not straightforward. There are only 30 places in the race and generally the organisation favour past competitors (who know what they are letting themselves in for, should stay safe and will have likely already built up an on-line following). This means that in reality there are only around 10 places really open for new competitors and these are very keenly fought over.

On the one hand the X-Alps race is so extreme that it is, to a certain extent, self-selecting. In other words there are probably less than 100 people that can or want to put together a really convincing application. Even so, the odds are not great then if we leave it to luck. Not really believing in luck I set about doing some serious research on how to get selected. In my case this was quite easy as Tom Payne had run the race in

2009 and was able to share his experiences.

Over a number of beers in the pub opposite the main train station in Geneva we worked through what the selection committee would be looking for. In our opinion they wanted someone who was a safe bet. This race was after all a marketing event for Red Bull and a serious accident would be extremely bad for the race. In order to demonstrate that I would be safe as a competitor I needed to show that I was a very experienced pilot. With 20 years of flying experience up to world cup level, I had a good start on this one. But I needed a bit more. None of the organising committee knew who I was so I needed to find a way of convincing them that not only was I experienced but that I had the right attitude and frame of mind for this race. In order to do this I needed to find people known and trusted by the race selection committee who also knew me well, who would be able to provide references for my character and my flying. As I knew many previous X-Alps athletes and a number of well-known people in the sport from my varied career as a pilot, this was not too hard, but it still needed to be set up. I found out who was on the selection committee, found out who knew them and asked them to send emails recommending me. This meant that they had a little more information to go on than just what was on my application – they also had the word of a number of trusted pilots known to them. Secondly they were looking for people with the right fitness and mountain experience. Fitness I could demonstrate, but despite having outdoor sports in my blood, I had to admit that I didn't have any real big mountain experience (skiing, snowboarding and hiking didn't really seem to count for much against ski-tourers, mountaineers and mountain guides!) I knew this would count against me, so I had to make sure I did a good job on the last count. As this is a marketing event they also need pilots who want to share their experiences, who have a name and a following. I'd been in and out of national level competitions over the last few years and whilst I was reasonably well known and respected in the British paragliding scene, I was little known outside of it. Hence I started, from spring 2010, to write a blog of my flying and training. By the time the race opened for applications, there was a reasonable following and a number of interesting stories up. An interesting side effect of this exercise was that it kindled a joy of writing I wasn't previously aware of, which has culminated in putting this book together!

Applications closed at the end of September and then began the long wait. Finally in the last week of October the race website stated that next Monday would be the announcements – just one more weekend to find out quite how disrupted the next 10 months of my life would be. Monday morning came and an email arrived. I was a reserve. I was gutted – this was worse than a 'no', at least then I could have got on with my life. Being a reserve felt terrible – committing to all the training and preparation that would be needed seemed nearly impossible knowing that there was a high chance I would not be starting the race. I called the organising committee and asked what being a reserve meant – how many were there and where was I on the list. It turned out that there were only three but that I was the third of the three! Finally I decided that I would keep training 'full-on' until Christmas and if I wasn't in by Christmas, I'd put the race behind me and do something else with my life!

Well, that was all emotional enough, but a month later the story took another twist. The organisation called me again to tell me they'd decided they were going to let two more athletes in (making a starting line-up of 32) given the risk of training injuries causing people to drop out. They'd called the two athletes in front of me on the reserve list, an Austrian and a French pilot, and offered them both the places. The Austrian accepted. He was Paul Guschlbauer who then went on to finish in third place overall. However, the French athlete had already made other plans and declined the offer. They called me to explain all this to me, but then told me that they were not giving me the place that would have gone to the French pilot but rather they would let me be the only reserve so if anyone else dropped out I'd be in. This was even worse – I was still a reserve and somehow the rules seemed to be different for me than for the other reserves. I wasn't really angry but I was rather upset. The nice lady who explained all this suggested I called Hannes Arch, the mastermind behind the race and still clearly one of the key decision makers. I thought I ruined my chances as I got rather emotional on the phone to Hannes. I don't know why really, I guess there was just so much at stake here, and I felt like I'd been treated unjustly. I thought getting upset on the phone was unprofessional , but as it turned out Hannes called me back later that day to tell me he'd talked to the rest of the committee and they had finally decided to let me in. Maybe the emotion helped after all! So with that roller coaster behind me I could now concentrate on getting ready. The irony was that in spring two people did drop out, both due to injuries and that in the end Paul and I finished in 3rd and 5th place respectively, not bad for a couple of reserves!

Time

I have the good fortune to know a chap called John Doerr, who is a former coach for an America's Cup team. During a discussion with John he gave me one piece of advice that turned out to be the most relevant, useful and practical piece of advice I have ever received! It was quite simply this: the most important asset in the preparation for something like this is time. Particularly in my case, with a full time job and a family, the most limited resource I'd have would be my own time. The point of this is that there are literally hundreds of things you can spend your time on when preparing for this race, far more things in fact that you have time for, probably by many multiples. Hence I needed to make choices; I needed to decide early on what I was going to focus on and, importantly, what I was not going to focus on. I decided that I would have three priorities. Firstly, I would focus on physical fitness, secondly on learning the route and finally on getting the right equipment together. But even within these there were choices to be made on how to go about it. For example, in order to learn the route I decided to spend my time on the ground travelling around the Alps as much as was possible and I would not spend a lot of time studying other peoples track logs or 'airways' charts (which are maps of popular flying routes in the alps). More on the logic behind this below.

Physical Preparation

I deem myself to be quite fit. At the time of entering the X-Alps I was cycling 20km every day (to work and back) and running about 3 times a week. I started from the point of view that this would give me a good base fitness, but it was a drop in the ocean compared to where I needed to be. In late summer 2010 I started to extend the distance I ran, doing longer runs at the weekend with my sights set on the Lausanne Marathon at the end of October. I figured if I could take part in a 864km race then a 42km one should be a walk in the park, more or less. That turned out to be rather naïve. I was quite fit, but I was also rather stubborn. About 20km into the race I could feel my knee starting to hurt. This seemed strange – I'd run much further than this before without a problem, so I ignored it and kept pushing on. Around 25km the runner behind me became very concerned when my knee actually buckled underneath me at one point. I stretched a little and pushed on. I was in a lot of pain but too stupid to stop. I finished the marathon in a slow 3hr42mins, it was my first marathon and clearly it hadn't been too bright a thing to do.

I'd injured my IT band on the outside of my right knee. I was extremely concerned as I'd had a recurrent knee injury a few years before and I was scared this would come back. As it turned out it just needed rest – a lot of rest – weeks of it in fact. With hindsight this experience was probably a very good wake up call, because it made me listen to my body and be much more cautious about my training from that point on. I took it very easy until late December when everything seemed back to normal and I started gradually ramping up the running again.

My only other training injury was a mild calf strain which I recognised immediately and stopped running for two weeks letting it heal straight away.

Running seems to be a very efficient way to get fit, but this race is not about running. It is about walking up mountains with a paraglider and it is about walking a long way during a day. A very mild winter allowed me to start doing exactly this as early as January – hiking up places and flying down. I started to learn new things – even shoes I had worn for weeks and runs 100's of kilometres in gave me blisters after ten kilometres walking. I began to realise that to be truly ready from a fitness point of view I had to be doing lots of training, but most importantly I had to be doing the right kind of training. I didn't actually know what the right type of training was – so it was time to get help!

About this time I went to a talk organised by my work's running club. The talk was given by Pierre Morath, an experienced marathoner, trainer and owner of a local specialist running shop. I emailed him afterwards to see if he could help me and went to see him the following Saturday morning. He explained the first task was to get a test done to find out where my various fitness thresholds were and find out my VO2 max. Pierre sent me to see Frederic Gazeau who would run the tests and build a training plan for me. After a lot of training I was pretty confident of my fitness and with this in mind I sat down with Frederic to talk through the results of the test. He explained what it all meant, how the body works and what is important for this kind of endurance race. It all made sense but I didn't have anything to compare the numbers, graphs and curves in front of me to. So I asked him, how did I look on paper to him? Was I in good shape? "Not for this kind of event" was his rather disappointing reply. Frankly I was a bit gutted but it motivated me to focus on what I needed to do to get better.

I'm no expert on training for events like this, which is

why I knew I needed someone who was. But it turns out that for endurance events you need to train your body to work very efficiently at low rates. This means 'teaching' the body to work of fat and not of sugars. Running above my anaerobic threshold was, in reality doing nothing for my endurance level. I had to change my training plan dramatically. I had to start *walking* places! Frederic set me up a new training regime, which built up across several monthly cycles but started as follows:

- 2 x per week 10km walk with heart rate always less than 110bpm (it had to be flat)
- 2 x per week 10km running with heart rate less than 150bpm
- 1 x per week interval training
  - o Warm up 10mins @ 140bpm, 10mins @ 155bpm, 10mins @ 165bpm
  - o 5 repetitions of 2mins at 15 km/h followed by 2mins at 12 km/h
  - o 20mins cool down jogging at 9 km/h
- Long distance walk (>3hrs) which could include gentle gradients, but with heart rate always below 130bpm

10kms is an important distance because it was the distance between my house and my office! In other words we built a realistic plan focussed as much as possible on training through my daily commute. I just needed to do one long walk at the weekend and the interval training on the other day, trying to keep one day free (ideally following the interval training) to rest and recuperate. In fact my rest days still involved cycling the 20km to work and back!

Looking at the above you might think this is a lot but actually it felt very easy compared to all the running I had been doing. Suddenly I was training much more at my base endurance level or just under my anaerobic threshold (13 km/h/167bpm) with only the interval training to really push the upper limit. And, boy, was the interval training hard! The thing Frederic was insistent about was avoiding steep hills. Again this seemed strange advice because I was going to have to get through the mighty Alps. When I quizzed him on it he told me simply, 'not yet, it will come'. Indeed later on in the training the long walk evolved in to a big alpine romp, sometimes covering as much as 70kms and always with a paraglider on my back.

The fact I knew nothing about physical conditioning at the start of this was the very factor that led me to get proper advice and in hindsight this was key to my success on the ground.

Equipment

Let's start with the basics. For this race I needed a paraglider. A quick chat with my friends at Ozone confirmed they'd support me. Having the backing of a manufacturer was very important in the 2011 race, not because I was on 'the scrounge' for a free wing (although Ozone did generously provide it free of charge) but because I needed a specially made wing for the race. It could be based on a standard production wing but it would need to be made from lightweight materials. That is to say lighter weight fabric, skinny, lightweight risers and even small loops of dyneema replacing the normal metal maillons attaching the risers to the suspension lines. This was all achieved by Ozone with a wonderful attention to detail. The real choice to be made though, and one I agonised over, was which wing would my 'lightweight special' be based on? Pilots in this race used all levels of glider from EN B (basic intermediate) up to open class competition wings. For me the real choice was between the Mantra M4, a certified high performance sports wing and the R11, Ozone's full on competition wing, and by a large margin, the best performing production wing on the market at that time.

The problem with the R11, if it could be called a

problem, is that whilst it was relatively easy to fly it was a handful to launch and to land. Furthermore, whilst it is a very solid and stable wing it also has a reputation for being very challenging to recover if it does collapse. I reasoned, correctly as it turned out, that I'd be flying in some of the most demanding and extreme conditions that would be possible and having to launch and land in some very tight places. So after much deliberation and worry that I'd be being left behind on booming XC days (finally not an issue), I opted for the M4. I think almost all the other Ozone pilots made a different choice, instead choosing the R11. In the final analysis though only one of them (Martin Müller) actually beat me!

So, next to the harness. Initially I thought this would be a bigger challenge, but in the end it all rather dropped into place. I tested the Advance Lightness and a few others before I got to know Clement Latour, also competing in the race. Clement works at Sup'Air and was developing a special harness for the race. Sup'Air is based just down the road from me in Annecy. Whilst the Lightness is a great harness, the support from Advance would only go as far as providing a standard harness at trade price (weight 2.3kg, whereas Maurer's special version from Advance was probably closer to 1kg). By contrast, at Sup'Air I got to fly the early prototype and influence, albeit a little, how my final harness turned out. Those prototypes soon evolved into what is now the Sup'Air Delight. Apart from the great working relationship with the team at Sup'Air, the Delight was comfortable and well built, and below 2kg it was about the lightest pod harness I could find available.

For the rest of the minimum flying equipment the key criteria was weight – light helmet, lightweight emergency flare and a single combination instrument to fly with.

But flying equipment was only part of the story. I needed poles to walk with, and found some great lightweight Gipron ones (although, if you've already read the book you'll know I broke one of them 2 days from the finish, perhaps they were too light after all!). I also needed to think carefully about clothing. I'd often need to walk many hours up with my full flying clothing. Being warm in the air was critical and getting it wrong was punishing physically and tough on morale. I ended up investing in a high quality down jacket, light but exceptionally warm, and the combination of this with the lightweight waterproof provided by race sponsors Bergens kept me warm in the air.

Looking after my feet was an even more serious undertaking. By the end of my training I was covering 150km each week by foot, and this meant I got though plenty of pairs of trail shoes. As the race approached, I realised I'd need to invest in new shoes a month or so prior to the race so that I could break them in but not wear them out. I went back to New Concept Sports in Geneva, the same people who had helped me sort out a proper training plan for the race. I spent an entire morning with Laurent Paonessa who runs the Geneva shop. Laurent patiently got me to try on shoe after shoe, each time running around the block, and often with different shoes on each foot, in order to make sure the shoes were exactly right. The terrace dwellers in the café next door, enjoying their espressos in the spring sunshine seemed quite amazed after I ran past them time after time with oddly matching shoes in increasingly ridiculous colours. The effort was worth every Swiss Franc and every minute as having the right shoes was one of the keys to making sure my feet stayed in good condition. They were not the only contributor though.

Asking previous X-Alpers about blisters led to all sorts of stories about how to treat blisters, draining them, dealing with them and so on. At least, all but one. Rumour had it that Honza Reijmanek had a magic solution for blisters. So I got in contact with him. He told me he didn't mind sharing his secret as he felt all the gory images of nasty blisters were quite distracting from the race. I hope he really meant it as I am now sharing his secret with the world! His solution was simple. He used a product called Friction Zone, made by a company ... wait for it ... called Brave Soldier (no, really). The product is simply a water based lubricant that you rub on your feet. It prevents blisters forming and doesn't damage your socks like an oil based lubricant (such as Vaseline) will. Keeping my feet clean, dry and lubricated with Brave Soldier was the key to a virtually blister free race.

The final trick in the 'looking after the feet' puzzle was socks. There are some excellent running socks out there, and I have a lot of pairs, but they are not actually ideal for walking long distance, especially in rain or hot weather (leading to sweaty feet). On this one my Dad had the solution from his experiences from the Mt Blanc Ultra Trail and the Marathon de Sables – wool socks. Sounds rather old fashioned but the modern 'smart wool' variety are excellent at wicking away water and sweat and keeping my feet dryer for longer. A whole drawer full of these and we were set up on the feet front!

So far so good? Not quite. We are missing one rather key piece of equipment, and the object that is the biggest expense for most teams: the camper van. Not only is it the biggest expense but also it could easily become the biggest absorber of time. Many teams converted normal vans or mini-buses, saving expense but taking up a lot of time. Time was something I did not have. From the beginning I had not been too focussed on having my equipment covered by sponsors, where they were willing I gladly accepted their support and provided the necessary exposure for their great products. But I prioritised getting the right equipment over getting free equipment meaning in many cases I just went and bought what I needed. The van was different though. If we were going to be well equipped and comfortable during the race we needed a modern well equipped van. This was beyond my budget for the race so this was where I needed to get a sponsor. I was lucky here too, I put together a proposal and after a few discussions with the brand manager for Pringles Xtreme, it was clear they were open to support me and the costs for the van were within the amount they considered covering. In hindsight I was very smart with my request – smarter than I realised at the time, because I asked them not only to fund the van but to take over finding, hiring and preparing it. This was in their own interest because the deal was they could cover the van in whatever livery they wanted (with the exception only of the two front doors which needed to be left free for the race logos). By letting them take ownership of selecting, hiring, and decorating the van it took away from me a whole heap of work contacting potential rental companies. All I did was write a brief for the type of van we needed and when we needed it from and to and a lovely lady from their agency took care of all the rest. Their generosity meant we were able to have the van for a month before the race. This turned out to be ideal because we were able to do many of our training trips in the van. In the process we resolved all the niggly little 'bugs' like having all the equipment stowed in the most convenient places or which types of meals are easy to prepare in the limited space for cooking. Having all of this stuff sorted out before we were even in the race, is, I am sure, one of the reasons we were able to do so well in the race itself.

Learning the route

Nobody can know the entire Alpine region inside out. It is massive. There is a temptation to therefore say, it doesn't really matter, as long as I know how to read a map and how to fly in mountains, I'll be fine. This was not true.

When I started to analyse the route in detail it was quickly clear that, whilst there were multiple route choices, for the most part they could be analysed and narrowed down to just a few important ones. But it is remarkable, in hindsight, how difficult this is to do from a map. Dad and I set aside almost every long weekend between spring and summer, as well as a week and half holiday, to simply travel the route in chunks and learn the area. I flew wherever I could, testing equipment at the same time. This also enabled me to change my mind from a cross country pilot, to an X-Alps pilot, where simple top to bottom flights can be as important as big cross-country flights. Where the route followed valleys there was no need to walk the course, but where it had to cross mountain ranges there were typically few options, so I walked almost every mountain pass in practise that I'd end up walking in the race. We drove every valley and every col with a road through it. We ran up the mountain from the top of the Simplon Pass in spring snow to peer down into the Zermatt valley and check if there were take-off options. But just as importantly we learnt where the shops were on the route, sections where there were few opportunities to get fuel, which days it was impossible to buy stuff in which countries and so on. Even simply knowing which logos were supermarkets in which countries helped because by the time we came to the race it was all familiar.

In these training trips we got lost. I flew down the wrong valley in the Dolomites, we almost went down the wrong valley from Bormio and on one occasion we lost each other completely (my fault – I left my cell phone in the car when I took off and my radio battery was flat!). We went completely the wrong way walking on top of the Dachstein glacier and had to retrace our steps losing about an hour. I even landed backwards in horrendous valley winds and discovered more or less unlandable tracts of valley. Each time we learnt something, and we did not make these same errors in the race. We knew the towns, we knew their names and we each had a mental map of the narrow tract of the Alps we'd be passing through. Put simply, by the time the race started we knew where we were going.

But back to the route choices. There were a few places in the race where there were what I call 'macro choices'. The two that stand out were the section from Piz Palu to the top of lake Como (day 8) and the section from Bellinzona to the Matterhorn (days 9 & 10). Dad and I had visited the Bernina

Pass and the section around Piz Palu twice in training. There were three possible scenarios here. The first one was that I would take the turn point in the air on a great flying day and I'd be able to fly due west along the mountains. This was easy, if conditions were right it was the simple and most direct choice. However we had to prepare for all eventualities. So options 2 and 3 were rather more likely. Option 2 was to go south down to the Sondrio valley and then out west. Option 3 was up and over the Bernina Pass to the north and into the St Moritz valley. We spent some time checking this one because it was not immediately obvious. On closer study though the North route was 20km shorter if it all had to be walked and the total height gain to the next line of mountains (west of Chiavenna) was actually less because the Sondrio valley was at such a low altitude. What's more, the St Moritz valley was mostly devoid of trees, allowing me to launch more or less anywhere I needed to. By contrast we spent some time trying to find launchable spots high above the Sondrio valley without much luck – you needed to get above the tree line and it was a height difference of about 1500m – one heck of a trek! The conclusion? If I had to walk it I was better off going north, if there was a chance I could fly, I was better off going north. Hence I eliminated a possible decision point in the race through detailed planning – whatever happened here I'd go north! Incidentally, only Thomas De Dorlodot and I went this way in the race (and we gained as much as half a day to a day's lead versus the people just behind us who went south). In the race the weather was terrible and the 'easy' choice looked like simply descending to Sondrio. What I learnt from this is how difficult it is to make rationale and data based decisions in the heat of the race without the necessary planning and preparation.

By contrast there were at least 3 perhaps 4 routes between Bellinzona and Zermatt. I'd studied these in detail (except the most southerly one that Martin and Paul took in the race) and finally decided the choice would need to be made on the day as the weather would be the most significant determining factor. Still, having flown parts of each of them and driven all of them I had a good feeling for the choice when I had to make it on what turned out to be one of the best flying days in the race. When it came to it in the race I took the longest route, round to the north and through the Neufenen pass. It did not gain me much time on people who went the other way, but I did manage to fly most of it and avoided the punishing 3000m ascent up on to the Monte Rosa glacier.

So learning the route for us was all about being familiar with the terrain, knowing the terrain and understanding where there were choices on that route and what factors would influence those choices.

Appendix 2: Paragliding terms for non-pilots

This section gives a brief explanation of the paragliding terms used in the text for non-pilots. Terms are explained in more or less the order they appear in the main text.

Turn points are the locations we need to pass during the race. Each turn point consists of the co-ordinates of the point itself and a radius representing how close we need to get to the exact point. In the race this radius varied from 1km to 5km. To have reached the turn point our live tracking device simply had to record a data point inside this virtual cylinder.

Thermals are bubbles of hot air that rise from ground level on sunny days. They are caused by the sun heating the ground which in turn heats the air close to it, this air becomes warmer than its surroundings until it 'unsticks' from the ground and rises up through the rest of the air. Circling in a thermal is the primary way in which paragliders gain altitude.

Stability refers to a situation where there are very few thermals, or the thermals that are created quickly stop ascending. This occurs when the air temperature does not drop sufficiently with altitude. In stable conditions it is very difficult to gain altitude.

Drift refers to the distance travelled over the ground when circling in a thermal. With no wind the drift would be zero, as we climbed we'd stay over the same spot, but if there is some wind we are 'drifted' downwind as we climb.

Headwinds and tailwinds relate to the direction of the wind versus the direction of travel. A paraglider has a more or less constant speed relative to the air, but once there is some wind the air we are moving through is itself moving. This is just the same effect as swimming in a river – if you go with the current you move quickly but going against the current is much harder work! Hence with a tailwind we can cover more distance over the ground with the same altitude and do so at a faster speed, whilst with a headwind we are resigned to making slower progress than would be typical and losing more altitude for every meter travelled over the ground.

Glide angle refers to the ratio between the distance we cover and the height we lose. This is important because paragliders are always sinking through the air, however in doing so they also travel forwards. A glide angle of 8:1 means for every 8m we cover over the ground we lose 1m. My glider in the competition had a glide angle of about 10:1 in still air.

Clouds. Everyone knows what a cloud is, but, on the other hand entire text books have been written on the topic! Mostly in this book I refer to cumulus clouds, the white fluffy clouds you see on a nice sunny day. These mark the top of the thermals, because it is the warm parcel of air rising that contains the water vapour which condenses into the cloud. In the first chapter I refer to **threatening clouds** which is where the cumulus clouds grow into much bigger clouds and in doing so either spread out (cutting off the heat to the ground and stopping the thermal activity required to sustain flight) or turn into a storm, where the cloud creates its own energy and becomes unstable, meaning it will grow extremely quickly and without warning. Such storms can be very dangerous for paragliders. This is why I referred to the clouds as 'threatening'!

This situation where the clouds build very fast and can cover the sky or storm is often referred to as **overdevelopment.**

Circling is simply what we do to stay in the narrow column of lifting air that is a thermal, and hence go up. Normally even a large thermal will have a stronger 'core' so we tend to circle quite tightly to climb as fast as possible.

The **speed bar**, or **accelerator** is a bar we can push with our feet which is attached via a pulley system to the front of the paraglider. By pulling down on the lines that link us to the leading edge of the wing, it decreases the angle at which the wing is at relative to the airflow and so increases the speed we travel through the air. One side effect of this can be to make the wing more unstable, or at least to make any collapses due to turbulence both more likely and more difficult to deal with.

Air is always moving around, and even when there are no thermals there can be areas of **lifting air.** A typical cause can be **convergence** where two airflows meet – in this situation the air has to go up as it has nowhere else to go. Similarly there can also be areas of **sinking air.** Just as headwinds and tailwinds affect our glide over the ground so does lifting or sinking air. Gliding through strongly sinking air will reduce the distance we are able to travel significantly.

'Big Ears' is a configuration of the glider where we deliberately fold in the wing tips on both sides to give a smaller wing area and therefore increase our sink rate through the air.

If big ears are not sufficient to descend quickly enough then we will often **spiral down** by doing very tight turns with the glider banked up on its side.

Rotor refers to air which rolls over in a type of eddy. If wind passes over a sharp obstacle, such as a knife-edge ridge, then it will curl over forming rotor rather like a surfer's ideal wave. Unlike the surfer on his wave though, rotor is generally to be avoided on a paraglider as it brings severe turbulence and strongly sinking air.

Risers are the short section of webbing that attaches the harness to the suspension lines which in turn are connected to the fabric wing of the paraglider. We use the risers to launch the wing and to control it on the ground.

There are two main techniques of launching a glider mentioned in the book. The first one is a **forward launch** which involves facing the direction of take-off holding the risers in each hand. As you run forward the wing comes above your head and then you are able to run off the hill. This works well for light winds. In stronger winds it is preferable to use the **reverse launch** where you start facing the wing. This technique allows better control of the wing as you bring it above your head, but of course the risers are twisted so you need to turn around before actually taking off.

A **downslope wind** is pretty self-explanatory, but is relevant because to launch a paraglider it is normally necessary to have the wind blowing up the slope rather than down. As soon as the wind blows down the slope it makes the launch very difficult. To illustrate this – imagine there is a light 10 km/h wind up the slope and the glider needs a speed of 25 km/h to fly. To launch with the wind coming up the slope you need to only to run at 15 km/h to reach the required 25km/h air speed the wing needs – fast but easily manageable on a slope. With the same light wind blowing down the slope you now need to reach 35km/h before launching which is rather more challenging!

Katabatic flow refers to where the cool air on the higher ground (generally at night) slides down the slopes and valleys because it is heavier than the surrounding air. This is exactly the opposite effect to the thermals and upslope winds we rely on for much of our flying.

A **variometer,** or **vario** for short, is an instrument that tells us how quickly we are ascending or descending through the air via beeps that change in pitch and rapidity. In the race I carried a combination instrument which included GPS, altimeter and variometer in one device.

A **parachutal stall** is where the glider is behaving like a parachute rather than a glider, that is to say it is falling vertically through the air rather than gliding through it. In a parachutal stall the wing stays open but is no longer moving forwards.

Printed in Great Britain
by Amazon